D1641499

POEM
ON
ALGIERS

DIE POESIE ALGIERS

LE CORBUSIER

POEM
ON ALGIERS

DIE POESIE ALGIERS

Postface by Cleo Cantone
Nachwort von Cleo Cantone

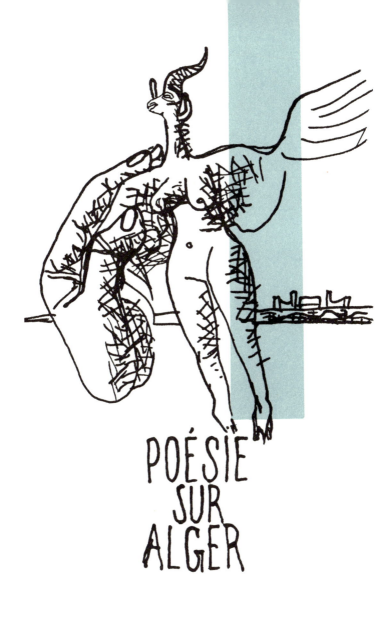

POÉSIE
SUR
ALGER

Max Pol Fouchet instructed me to write for *Fontaine*.

Fontaine is a harbor open to the poetic vessels of a France stunned by the consequences of a hellish defeat—France on her knees, one fine day, after having repeatedly let herself be bullied by the great boorishness of the end of the first machine era, which was dominated by merchants; the pure and the fervent were no longer highly rated in this market. A nauseating fair, a trumped-up comedy, academism at its command posts (eternally old, permanently dilapidated). From these circumstances arises the providential reestablishment of values inciting to thought, poetry, lyricism, exploring, to be instigators, to be movers, to appoint a direction to the trajectory to the enterprise of regeneration, to extract the country's effort from mediocrity, to uplift the forces of enthusiasm, the impulses of one's heart, to provoke these disinterested, free gestures that are the spice of life, which are, in the end, happiness itself, radiance, contentment. Lifting men above platitudes and opening up before them the path of discovery of the heart, where each is his own master, free reaper of the riches found in life.

This is a topical point of view. It is through this that the real objects of valid consumption will appear. Poetry, leading player of the economic and mistress of the social sphere. We know well (and our times prove it) that the voltage of a society consists of feelings. Feelings place you on a certain level and from this altitude comes the appreciation of things.

Urban planning is precisely the expression of a society's vitality. In the whole world, a show without ambiguity is chaos, recklessness, and confusion. Mediocrity of lives and days, cities without hope, in Europe and in America. How to overcome such disgrace? Cities are sick with the plague . . .

They are sick because poetry has left the heart of their crafts generations ago. Architecture and architects have fallen to the lowest depths. The engineer, master and usurper, has covered the planet with his inventions. These inventions—descendants of impassive calculation, the very calculation of the laws of nature—were not in any way uplifted by an enlightening virtue: harmony. No, they were clothed in pretentiousness; some courses in architecture have besmirched working drawings. So many horrors tarnished Algiers back then, just as they tarnished Paris.

Thirteen years of perseverance and dogged work and a certain opportunity led me here in the spring of '42 to bring the managers the fruit of a long meditation: a *master plan* (2). A "master plan" for Algiers and its surroundings.

The word is new; the thing is new. It is the ferment of the future injected in the middle of factual chaos, capable of directing people's behavior—joy having been reintroduced into the heart of the primordial cell, the family, civil mindedness, syn-

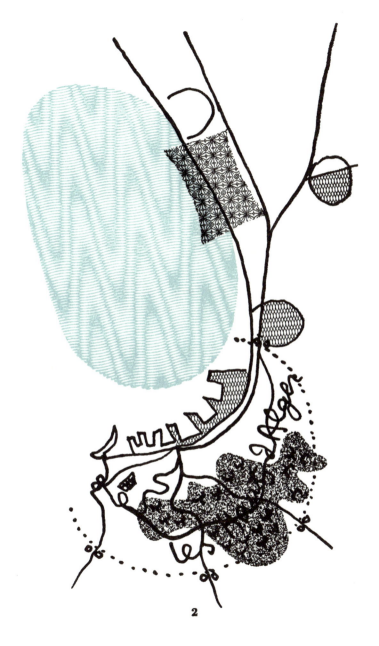

2

thetic result of enthusiasm, of trust and faith, inscribed in community work, giving businesses their irresistible strength, their irresistible force, preparing the brilliant city for the drab setbacks of our times.

Poetry radiates over Algiers: a master plan—the master plan—will make this apparent.

It is not subjective at all but steeped in North-African reality. Freed from rules, the master plan confirms that the sources of profoundly human joy will spread if the site's resources are placed at the people's service (3). For fifteen years I have classified these joys as "essentials": sun, space, greenery. "Essential joys."

espace

le sol naturel

3

We are in Africa. This sun, this expanse of blue and sea, this greenery, are what enveloped Salambo's mournful gestures, the actions of Scipio and Hannibal as well as those of Kheir-ed-Din Barbarossa. The sea, the chain of the Atlas and the mountains of Kabylia display their auspicious blues. The earth is red. The vegetation consists of palms, eucalyptuses, gum trees, cork oaks, olive trees, and prickly pears; the perfumes of jasmine and mimosa. From the foreground to the boundaries of the horizon, a symphony is immanent.

By building their Casbah (4), the Turks had attained a masterpiece of architecture and urbanism. But the last fifty years of European colonialism abolished the adjoining natural richness and remorselessly petrified

the new city into a rubble desert
whose tightly packed houses lean
over noisy streets. The inhabitants
cram onto the pavements on their
practically sole Isly Street—Michelet
Street[1]—parading between the rented walls with charmless gait, in the
beautiful hours when the abating
evening air fills with sweetness (5).
From the windows of their rooms,
except for a few evaders, they face
nothing but walls, and these too are
pierced by windows that look back at
them.

.   .   .   .

I decided to cut through these
neighborhoods, guided by instinct.

I cut through the built chaos and
climbed straight up, following the
steepest slope of the cliff, trampling
the indefatigable steps between

le Dedans

le Dehors

4

houses whose doors feed into as many storeys below as above (skyscrapers barbarously erected in contempt of building regulations) or through well-kept alleys, linking, for those who know their way around, the sea to the point culminating with the slopes, at Fort-L'Empereur,[2] at two hundred and fifty meters' altitude. Jacob's ladder, bearing the pretty name of Lys du Pac. At height 100, you cross the path along the old Turkish aqueduct, clinging to the cliff's crevices: the Télemly.[3] Then, with the Puyanne Path, the hike resumes, rapid, fruitful, full of recompense. The horizon has opened up, expanded; the field of vision is immense, set with snippets of sea or mountains between wings of eucalyptus or pine, and the vertiginous drop of the hills. Ewes and goats (6), occasionally donkeys, graze in rare pastures on rough ground. Down below, as if seen from a telescope, jagged by nearby foliage, liners appear in sections, their anchors waiting for the next peace treaties: black shells and white superstructures, red chimneys, blue sea, grey oars, and russet earth: paradoxical cut-out, where, on the same canvas, ravines hurtle down, tree vaults soar, the tides spread out. Prickly pears act as fences for indigenous huts. Here and there, above the enclosing wall, the radiant blossoming of a palm tree has taken the sea as a horizontal measurement.

In the twinkling of an eye we were brought here, in the blue, sea and sky commingled, in a miraculous and unhoped-for world, inhabited by fervent and distant Kabyles and emancipated Europeans who were after a

shed or a villa, reckoning that so much grandeur and such pure air are worth a daily sweat on the mountain road.

The inhabitants of Algiers do not come here, have never come here, would not and will never if . . .

. . . .

So I cut through the city, the thickness of two hundred meters of rented blocks with an assortment of trams, trolleys, and cars—down there, where people lurk. Then crossing another two hundred meters, as the crow flies, down rapid slopes, climbing rivulets, stairways (7).

I was on the "Heights of Algiers," that inestimable reserve, the place where the urban plans of tomorrow are going to take place, this street theater of the impending game of human habitation, the game of possible happiness of a society that has surpassed the black age of stupidity and hideousness, of laziness and carelessness, the new game of a herd that has found a few good shepherds.

This climb up the steepest line of the cliff is what I designate as one of the vertical axes of Algiers (8). The same goes for others that are just as pleasant, all along the cliff, leaning on the seashore, crossing the crust of nasty buildings, all opening onto the light . . .

This one touches the obelisk of Fort-l'Empereur, eminent landmark, white, emerging out of old brown walls. The brown stone was used in times gone by, effectively and beautifully by the Romans, then here, in this fort which does not belong to the emperor Napoleon III as one might

have thought, but to Charles V: the Casbah of the Barbary Coast was unassailable; on the island of the Admiralty at its feet, less than two hundred meters away, the Emperor lands and stations some canons; with other troops, having made a long crochet line along the bay, Cape Matifu and the cliff, he arrives at this culminating point, spot height 200, and two hundred meters from the Casbah, he builds a fort within range and adds more canons.

The length of two hundred meters is the same in longitude as in altitude, repeats itself strangely, marking the combined thickness and scale that suffice to blind the ways to happiness.

Two hundred meters away is beautiful land capable of satisfying the inhabitants who would consider

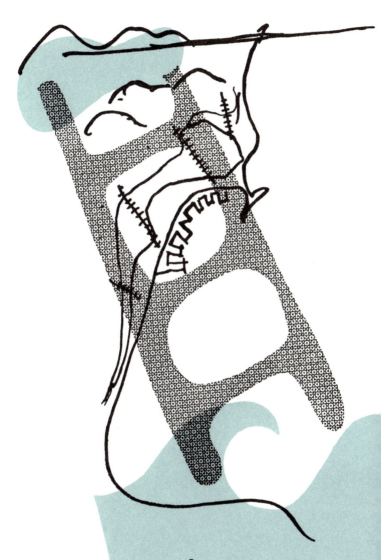

8

moving there! But they do not go there. They are packed in cages (9) of rented blocks of flats, where the air is bad and where you can't see anything, nothing at all: neither sea, nor boats, nor mountains, nor expanses, nor trees, nor red earth, nor anyone who knows how to have a good time.

I spoke to a mayor about this around 1930, proclaiming my discovery and proposing to install three hundred thousand people up there. He said: "Yes, yes . . . I've been past Fort-l'Empereur, when I was in the barracks, forty years ago . . ." And precisely in Algiers, in the city councils to be precise, and precisely at the time of this conversation, they were planning on building *a metro, underground,* to take people away from their parcels of land—to devil

knows where! They were also developing (10) plans for cardboard boxes to rent, at the feet of the Casbah, on the land "of the Marina" that had been reclaimed by demolishing slums. On the body of French Africa and on the very face of Algiers—yea, on the very nose of this face—renting boxes! On this great African soil!!! Misadventure! Recklessness! Carelessness! Destruction of poetical values! Murder of poets!

In these low-lying areas of the city, and on the edge of the waves, in this whole port fashioned out of embankments and ballasts, where salty water infiltrates, palm trees would be at ease, the tall palm trees of the oasis. In the forest, in the palm grove, swaying in the sea breeze and covering the entire port, planted in

10

the numerous "dead spots" neglected by handling crates, barrels, bundles and cases, coal and minerals. On the ground, a palm tree doesn't take up more than a footstool; twenty meters away it flourishes like a firework. The port of Algiers is lower down from the vast vaulted structures supporting the raised boulevard and arcades. The modern port today is nothing but a gash in the water of an engineer's working drawing: life swarms about there in the crowds of Africa's early produce and heavy goods, coal, and minerals. Abundance but also mediocrity of commercial transactions, money games. Between the pier of Kheired-Din (11) and the prow of Bastion 15 at Agha—a thousand meters in length—a solitary and unique palm tree balances, an old sage or an old

madman, with his superb foliage, born by chance; it suffices for him to rouse the poet in one, to suggest an idea, to encourage initiative. All alone in the port of Algiers, he is at once spirit, promise, radiance, and joy of the port; he dominates one's thoughts . . .

Mr. Prefect, a letter from you addressed to Messrs Engineers of the Department of Civil Engineering of Algiers, enjoining people to plant palm dates wherever there are "dead spots" between traffic and warehouses in the port, assuring you the most flattering recompense. In around twenty years' time they will say: "the palm trees of the Prefect of Algiers." They will line the port, encrust the stone jetty and docks[4] with cargos and ocean liners, battleships and tugboats, with the white sails of yachts, spreading a carpet of sweet, green swell at the city's feet adjoining the blue swell of the rising tide. Windy days, the white crests of the Mediterranean, and the rustling of the palm trees.

Hoisting and hauling machines will pass through; cheap, disparate merchandise that is loaded and unloaded will henceforth be no more than a secondary optical event . . .

We get to the heart of the *débat Algérois.*

We have already spoken about housing three hundred thousand people on the Heights and to spreading the palm trees under the city's footsteps (12).

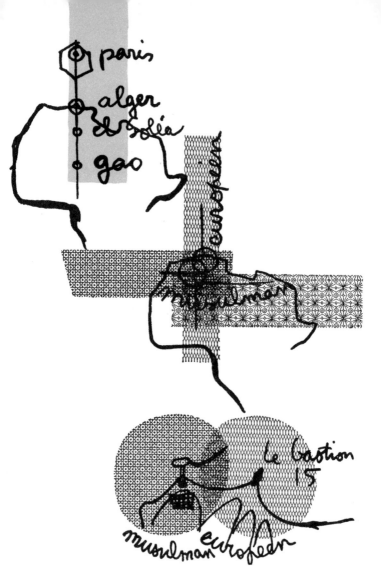

paris

alger

el biéa

gao

européen

musulman

le bastion
15

musulman européen

12

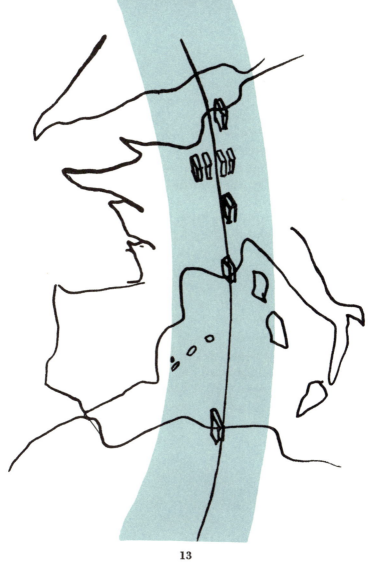

Algiers sticks to its thorny topography on the Paris meridian—El Golea—Gao, facing the sea, metropolitan France, Europe, a ribbon-like shore, narrow but sufficiently so to distinguish its touching traits, splendidly, magnificently architectural, harbingers of the French capital of Africa. At sea, the ships, from afar, will see it appear (13).

With its crescent-shaped harbor, Algiers considers itself *a city that looks at itself* (14). It's worth investing in architectural landmarks: noblesse oblige!

Now, fragmented, selfish views manipulations, prepare, on the contrary, asphyxiation from the cradle for this destiny that is nevertheless written in history, geography, topography? The district of the "Marina" is under threat? The cape of Algiers

habitat

affaires
centre civique
casbah

musulman

14

on the Paris meridian will become a sin of urban planning (15)?

As a well-informed pilgrim of this land of possible miracles, animated by a staunch faith after thirteen years engaged in releasing its urban potential, I came to speak to the Governor, the Prefect, the Mayor, addressing to each one the finer points of how to manage a town, a region, an Africa, telling them:

"Mr. Governor, Mr. Prefect, Mr. Mayor, poetry is in this place that is called Algiers, on this land of Africa where three successive great civilizations came: the Phoenician, the Roman, the Muslim. Vestiges, witnesses scattered all over warning us against the mediocrity of our mercenary transactions; they affirm that grandeur is always accessible so long as one thought reigns: ONE.

15

The page turns on the first destructive era of the machinist civilization; the second era opens onto fire, blood, adversity—the era of harmony. A thought can bind the threads of our actions, spread out over time and space, certain to lead them to unity.

The game is played the world over. These are not the Olympian gods who descend from their abode to accomplish humanly impossible feats. It is the men you are who will lead to Olympus, their name, their memory, their undertaking, by the quality of the initiatives and responsibilities that you take (16). It is in your hands: the fate of five hundred thousand inhabitants of the present and future Algiers; the splendor of this African France whose head—the capital—will be made into a gem by your

16

orders; you will enjoy the recognition of the motherland because you would have acted at a moment when others would have been content to deal with day-to-day matters; the people will be astonished when confronted with this phoenix of France, which, once again, and utterly pitiful, is reborn from its ashes . . .

Two hundred meters of layered houses to cross your mind and two hundred meters of altitude to conquer with an urban planning solution. To mold clay on this seashore, dulled potential in this site, to fill it with splendor and prevent—yes, in time and urgently—the possibility that, for the sake of cheap labor, it will be transfixed by stupidity and error!

Poetry is, at the end of the day, Mr. Governor, Mr. Prefect, Mr. Mayor,

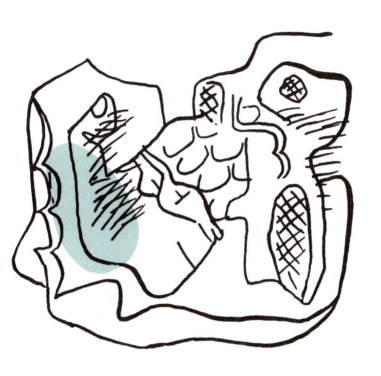

the essential nourishment of the
people; it's what gives endurance,
maintains courage, keeps the faith,
poetry is in Algiers, ready to enter,
to materialize in urban and architectural facts. Take control. It is still
not too late. Concentrate, unite, act!

Judgment will be severe one day,
if nothing is done efficiently, for we
will know the cause had been plead-
ed in time.

Algiers, May 1942.

EPILOGUE

PREFECT — Did you recognize the man who just left my office?

L.C. — Yes, it was Mr. Mayor.

PREFECT — He came here to make your arrest . . .

> In the session of June 12, 1942, the Municipal Council unanimously rejected the master plan of Le Corbusier.

"Poem on Algiers" could not appear in *Fontaine*. But the text and the thoughts contained here did find their visa, their papers, their typography, their platform,

nord-africains

avaux publics · Architecture · Urbanisme
et
urnée nord-africaine

ommerce — Agriculture — Industrie — Finances

Paraissant le Jeudi

35ᵉ Année
Nᵒ 1.998

Rédaction et Administration Centrales.
Publicité :
4, av. Pasteur, Alger
Tél. 596-25 et la nuite
Ch. Post. Alger 48-27

1 franc 75

1942
JEUDI
4
JUIN

Opinion d'antan restant d'actualité

L'architecture en péril

Dans son numéro du 5 mai 1934, La Libre Parole publiait sous ce titre un très intéressant article de Monsieur Alexandre de Senger. Les alliés de la juiverie internationale continuant, malgré les bouleversements, à intriguer sous des titres et des programmes différents pour accroître leur fortune et garder leur influence, cet article se trouve être encore d'actualité.
Nos lecteurs en jugeront.

N.D.L.R.

chose de plus que les corps de mᵗ tiers indépendants, elle fut l'expsion et l'animatrice de la fiede la gloire nationale. Sans thénon, point d'Athènes, sanr Dame, point de Paris, sans de Brandeburg, point de ᵖ monuments qui sont nᵈ ment d'honneur natᵗ par retour la rᵉ nés. De mémᵉ glaise au Sᵗ ment sur i

« Travaux Nord-Africains. — Bâtiment, travaux publics, architecture urbanisme». Nᵒ du jeudi 4 Juin 1942.

and their promoters. The Germans occupied Algiers just as they had Paris . . . The people who published these six columns on the first and last page of an important specialist newspaper took responsibility

en péril

reur du capitalisme bourgeois contre la résistance de l'architecture, et c'est pourquoi cette presse conspue tout ce qui est national, terroir, art, le sol et le sang, et voilà la cause pourquoi certains milieux bourgeois demandent la suppression des académies, pourquoi on appelle le style nouveau un danger, pourquoi l'on méprise Dante et Beethoven. L'on demanda la suppression des musées et la destruction des villes.

Le Corbusier ne se gêne nullement en faisant appel à la haute finance : il fait savoir que la destruction de Paris et de toutes les villes produirait une affaire magnifique pour l'industrie du béton, et pour les banques finançant les industriels de constructions nouvelles.

La réalisation de la construction nouvelle détruit tous les corps de métiers, et produit de nouvelles masses prolétaires. C'est ainsi que l'armée de non-bolchevistes est réduite et l'armée des bolchevistes agrandie... La construction nouvelle détruit la culture plastique, la peinture et la sculpture. Elle désanime l'homme et le réduit à l'animal géométrique. Elle ouvre aussi au capital international des débouchés énormes, et agrandit d'une façon gigantesque son omnipotence. L'on peut voir distinctement le développement en Russie où tout aboutit à la dictature d'un capitalisme d'Etat.

La construction nouvelle est le fait d'un capital anonyme, n'obéissant qu'à ses propres lois, étranger à tout sentiment de responsabilité, et ennemi de toute vie organique. Elle joue un rôle capital dont personne ne s'est rendu compte jusqu'à maintenant. Pour se réaliser, pour créer un marché artificiel, elle jette bas tout ce qu'englobe et résume le mot « architecture ». Amour du sol natal, sentiment national, sens historique famille passé et avenir. Elle dégrade l'architecture, l'abaisse au niveau d'un agent de banque ou d'industrie, elle ruine des centaines de milliers

d'artisans, elle détruit le cœur de la classe moyenne.

Nous constatons donc ici le plus gigantesque attentat contemporain perpétué par l'Internationale or et rouge. Nous sommes témoins d'une immense razzia faite par le capital anonyme avec l'aide et le secours du bolchevisme.

Cette entreprise gigantesque est organisée sous le nom de l'Association internationale pour la construction nouvelle. Douze nations font partie de cette association, entre autre les Soviets russes. C'est ainsi que le se-

municipaux de Moscou (Y.W. 14.114)

crétaire central de cette association qui dépend pour ainsi dire de Moscou trouve est

for suppression of an adversary who had only ever fought in the professional field of architecture and urban planning.

From 1930 to 1942 he offered the city of Algiers SEVEN successive master plans, free of charge. He had thus extracted the city and its services from its torpor. Starting from 1936, he had received a (benevolent) mission to represent the French government at the Commission of Planning of the District of Algiers.

In 1941, Emery[5] sent an SOS from Algiers, advising him that they were torpedoing the plan. Having resubmitted (once again, free of charge) his seventh plan to the prefecture, he had come in 1942 to break the silence . . . .

. . . .

Translator's notes

1   The rue d'Isly is now rue Ben Mehidi Larbi and is described in the *Guides Bleus Algérie Tunisie* (Paris, 1955, p. 58) as a bustling, commercial street with its neo-Moorish Bon Marché (1914). Rue Michelet (now rue Didouche Mourad), which turned into rue Péguy, joins rue Ben Mehidi Larbi; see *Guides Bleus Algérie Tunisie* (Paris, 1986, p. 75).

2   Fort-L'Empreur is now called Bourdj Moulay Hassan Pacha. See *Guides Bleus Algérie Tunisie* (Paris, 1974), p. 147.

3   Boulevard Télemly is where the aqueducts used to be, following the old Turco-Ottoman water pipes, which subsequently were restored; *Guides Bleus*, 1955 (see note 1), p. 80.

4   *Darse* or *darce* (in Italian darsena), the dock of a port, especially in the Mediterranean. From the *Larousse Illustré* (Paris, 1931).

5   Pierre-André Emery was "another Algiers-based architect of Le Corbusier's school"; see Zeinep Çelik, *Urban Forms and Colonial Confrontations: Algiers under French Rule* (Berkeley, CA, and London, 1997), p. 157.

FIN

POSTFACE
Le Corbusier and the Allure of Africa

Cleo Cantone

No stranger to controversy, Le Corbusier's political penchants have recently come under renewed scrutiny. In a book published this year, Xavier de Jarcy accuses the architect of promoting his theories in "aggressively anti-democratic" reviews. Of a somewhat misogynistic nature, Le Corbusier the artist "assaulted" Eileen Gray's modernist house on the Côte d'Azur with "a series of garish and ugly wall paintings, which he chose to execute completely naked."[1] Equally scathing are academic critiques of his promulgation of French supremacist discourse justifying colonization, in particular of the African continent. On the eve of the fiftieth anniversary of his death, the Centre Pompidou curator of a major exhibition of Le Corbusier's work claims that such criticisms are bent on discrediting the artist. Yet, incontrovertibly, Le Corbusier occupies the upper echelons of twentieth-century design. Along with global exhibitions of his work, there are numerous publications about him as well as reissues of his works, such as the present volume. The cult of modernism is far from dead.

As a *livre d'art,* Le Corbusier's *Poésie sur Alger* constitutes the expression of a vision, a dream in which urban planning embodies both the "cure" to poor urbanization and an aesthetic imperative ("Cities are sick with the plague").[2] One does not have to look far in the world's capitals for evidence of the "lack of poetry" Le Corbusier wrote about with such conviction: random erection of skyscrapers, demolition of listed buildings, and impingement on green spaces all contribute to the architect's rightful indignation, rendering his solutions—however contested—all the more credible. Indeed, Le Corbusier's letter to the prefect of Algiers could easily be addressed to the mayor of London today. In a similar vein to his contemporary compatriots, Le Corbusier aimed at preserving local, ancestral built forms and building modern—admittedly high-rise—business and residential quarters in an adjoining quarter. The tallest skyscraper planned for Algiers (plate 16), for example, does not completely obfuscate the mosque but rather acts as an imposing background (fig. 1).[3]

Since its appearance in print with Falaise in 1950,[4] *Poésie sur Alger* has been reprinted once in 1989 by Editions Connivences and more recently, in 2013, by the Algerian publishing house Éditions Barzakh. The present edition responds in part to Le Corbusier's desire to publish the "poem" in both French and English;[5] it is also driven by a desire to satisfy my own curiosity about what led this prolific Renaissance man to turn an aborted urban planning project into such a minutely formatted, poetic art book.[6] As Le Corbusier notes in his meticulously kept archives, the book's format should be "like Rilke 11/17 cm,"[7] and it constitutes his most diminutive publication. The 1989 dust jacket proclaims the book to be an ironic and

1   Skyscraper, marina quarter, business center, Algiers, February 1, 1939 / Wolkenkratzer, Hafenviertel, Geschäftszentrum, Algier, 1.2.1939
Black crayon on tracing paper / Schwarzer Farbstift auf Pauspapier, 93 x 110 cm

emotional reflection on Le Corbusier's thirteen years of unfruitful perseverance with his Algiers project. Described equally as "anachronistic and deceptive," what seems to have animated Le Corbusier's imaginative and creative energy was not only the redevelopment of the city, but also a more idealistic concept of Algiers as the embodiment of the future "Islamic pole" that would realign the balance of Mediterranean cultures. On the rear dust jacket of *Poésie,* the quadrilateral scheme was graphically illustrated thus:

Paris, Rome, Algiers, Barcelona. Writing to the mayor of Algiers, Mr. Brunnel, Le Corbusier explained that his poles conjoined the Channel to the Mediterranean, Europe to Africa: "Algiers ceases to be a colonial city" and becomes "the head of Africa. Its capital."[8]

With the backing of the minister of interior, Marcel Peyrouton, Le Corbusier put himself forward as the urban planner *par excellence* with a view to applying his theories on urbanism to the city of Algiers. Nevertheless, three urbanists had already proposed a master plan: René Danger, Henri Prost, and Maurice Rotival. Since the Marina quarter consisted of overcrowded, precarious buildings inhabited mostly by immigrants, this quarter was "neither Moorish, nor entirely European," according to René Lespès, who argued that the area needed cleansing on the grounds of poor hygiene.[9]

Aside from the urban planning dimension, *Poésie sur Alger* reveals an intimate aspect of Le Corbusier's personality that takes the form of a poetical farewell to a city he loved deeply. The love story began with his first trip to North Africa in 1931, coinciding with the celebrations of the centenary of "French" Algeria. Le Corbusier was invited to give two lectures for the Friends of Algeria society in March of that year on "The Architecture Revolution" and "The Radiant City."[10] Although these themes were at the forefront of the architect's mind, he was equally enchanted by Islamic architecture:

Arab architecture teaches us a very precious lesson. It favors walking, on foot; it's by walking, by moving on foot, that you can see the layout of architecture. It's a principle contrary to Baroque architecture which is conceived on paper, revolving round a fixed, theoretical point. I prefer the lessons of Arab architecture . . . They have managed to house so many so comfortably, in the various shadows of the courtyard, in the space of the terrace's horizons, because this Arab architecture holds the secret of human dimensions. These people, these terrible warriors, loved to rest well and knew how to savor *la joie de vivre*.[11]

A near contemporary, Carl Jung, visited Algeria and Tunisia with a friend in 1920:

This Africa is incredible . . . The Arab city is classical antiquity and Moorish middle ages, Granada and the fairy tale Baghdad. You no longer think of yourself; you are dissolved in this potpourri which cannot be evaluated, still less described: a Roman column stands here as part of a wall; an old Jewess of unspeakable ugliness goes by in white baggy breeches; a crier with a load of burnooses pushes past through the crowd, shouting in gutturals that might have come straight from the canton of Zürich; a patch of deep blue sky, a snow-white mosque dome; a shoemaker busily stitching away at shoes in a small vaulted niche, with a hot, dazzling patch of sunlight on the mat before him. . . . This is all nothing but miserable stammering; I do not know what Africa is really saying to me, but it speaks.[12]

Both authors refer to the "Arab" city and "Arab" architecture, yet neither seems to be consciously aware of the inaccuracy of this term: North Africans may be of mixed Arab blood, but the more unifying element of North Africa is surely Islam, the Arab element being little more than an ethnic component. Furthermore, the word may be substituted by Orientalism, defined by Edward Said as "a language whose institutional and disciplinary pres-ence eliminated, displaced the Oriental as human and put in his place the Orient Orientalized as specimen."[13] If Jung focuses on people's activities, Le Corbusier delights in the built and urban environment: both their descriptions fit with contemporary *tableaux,* using an Orientalist brush to portray the generic "Arab" who is capable of living a model of civilized life while displaying a bellicose side ("these terrible warriors") combined with a touch of childishness and irrationality:

Obviously, my encounter with Arab culture had struck me with overwhelming force. The emotional nature of these unreflective people who are so much closer to life than we are extorts a strong suggestive influence upon those historical layers in ourselves which we just have overcome and left behind, or which we think we have overcome. It is like the paradise of childhood from which we imagine we have emerged, but which at the slightest provocation imposes fresh defeats upon us. Indeed, our cult of progress is in danger of imposing on us even more childish dreams of the future, the harder it presses us to escape from the past. . . . The Arab's dusky completion marks him as a "shadow," but not the personal shadow, rather an ethnic one associated not with my personal but with the totality of my personality, that is, with the self. As a master of the Casbah, he must be regarded as a kind of shadow of the self // "my European consciousness."[14]

Rather than the confluence of three civilizations (Phoenician, Roman, and Muslim)[15] described in Le Corbusier's *Poésie sur Alger,* Jung smells blood in a soil that had "borne the brunt of three civilizations: Carthaginian, Roman, and Christian."[16] Whereas Jung's appreciation of North Africa is filtered through a dream about a confrontational encounter with a marabou and a visit to an imaginary medina, Le Corbusier transmits his vision in simple sketches, beautifully reproduced in the French edition of *Poésie sur Alger.* Yet at the root of Le Corbusier's attraction to the Algerian landscape and particularly its architecture, lies, no doubt what Jung portrays as "a childhood memory" that "takes possession of consciousness with so lively an emotion that we feel wholly transported back to the original situation, so these seemingly alien and wholly different Arab surroundings awaken an archetypal memory of an only too well known prehistoric past which apparently we have entirely forgotten."[17] Indeed, this archetypal memory evokes Le Corbusier's depiction of the mythological horned woman (*La femme à la licorne*) floating on the front cover of *Poésie sur Alger,* which he had previously used in *Le poème de l'angle droit* (fig. 2).[18]

Despite both authors' indisputable admiration for Arab (i.e. Muslim) civilization, the implication is that the indigenous Arab must, literally, stick to his feet for his means of transport and to the medina as his only possible dwelling space. The transformation of Algiers into a radical modernist paragon was in fact not radical at all, but instead bent on keeping the "charming," unchanging, "traditional" indigenous quarter intact while totally transforming the European business quarter. A text that lucidly exemplifies this point through its use of capital letters reads as follows:

2   *Hand, Licorne, and Landscape / Hand, Einhorn und Land-schaft*
Graphite pencil, black ink on paper / Grafitstift, schwarze Tinte
auf Papier, 30.5 x 24.7 cm

ALGERIAN, YOUR CAR CAN NO LONGER
DRIVE BECAUSE PARKING CLOGS UP YOUR
ROADS. ONE MUST THEREFORE PROHIBIT
YOU FROM PARKING, BUT THEN YOUR CAR
WILL BECOME USELESS AND USELESS TOO
ITS SELLER, YOUR GARAGE-MAN, YOUR RE-
PAIR-MAN, YOUR GASOLINE SELLER, YOUR IN-
SURANCE MAN.[19]

The preservation of the "authentic," "ado-
rable" medina served the metropolitan
goal of developing tourism while at the
same time serving as a justification for re-
ducing overcrowding: "one can design
and one can never, never destroy!"[20] To
this end, Le Corbusier proposed to con-
vert some residences into centers for arts
and crafts in an attempt to stoke a "renaissance" of local arts and crafts which
would in turn increase their commercial
value. Slums were to be cleared to make
way for parks and public gardens, but the
street network would be maintained to
link the high Casbah with the marina and
the harbor. Le Corbusier embraced the
separation of the indigenous and European towns, essentially trapping the medina

in a timeless capsule that embodied everything old, traditional, and stagnant, and stood in stark contrast to the new, modern, progressive European city. The two sections would be linked by the "business and civic center" (fig. 3).

Although not explicitly stated, Le Corbusier's vision for the "capitale française d'Afrique" would not be entirely rid of racial segregation, as illustrated by the plate showing the mosque perched on the tip of Algiers Bay, which is marked "musulman" and lies adjacent to the Casbah (plates 12, 14). Following the 1942 Athens Charter, the "ideal" city would be functionally segregated and people would live in widely spaced apartment blocks, which Le Corbusier's critics called "buildings in a car park" at best; at worst, a "Trojan horse of bolshevism."[21]

The 1938 sketches of the *plan directeur* depict the marina, with its wedge-like skyscrapers situated between the Casbah and the sea, as a barrier between what would become the business center

3   Urbanism, Algiers / Urbanismus, Algier, 1930
Black and blue crayon on paper / Schwarzer und blauer Farbstift auf Papier, 56 x 88 cm

(*cité d'affaires*) and the Muslim institutions. The "cement city" is therefore separated from the "white city" (fig. 4). Zeinep Çelik has written an insightful article exploring Le Corbusier's under-investigated "infatuation with Islamic culture" in the context of "19th century French discourse on the 'Orient' as well as the Parisian avant-garde's preoccupation with the non-Western Other in the 1920s and 1930s."[22] Indeed, the author characterizes Le Corbusier's travelogue of Istanbul as a standard traveler's view based upon the city's numerous foreign visitors across the ages, adding cryptically, "[h]e knew what he wanted to see." To the Orientalist Théophile Gautier, for instance, Algiers appeared as a "whitish blur" when he approached it from the sea. In a similar vein, Le Corbusier remarks: "The Casbah of Algiers . . . has given the name Algiers-the-White to this glittering apparition that welcomes at dawn the boats arriving at the port. Inscribed in the site, it is irrefutable. It is in consonance with nature."[23]

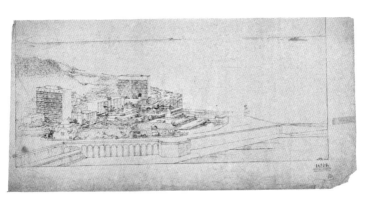

4   Skyscraper, marina quarter, business center, Algiers, February 24, 1939 / Wolkenkratzer, Hafenviertel, Geschäftszentrum, Algier, 24.2.1939
Heliotype on printing paper, Heliotypie auf Fotopapier, 89 x 110 cm

Le Corbusier's appraisal of Istanbul singles out the "cubic masses covered by domes," concluding that "great architecture is cubic," and he later sees the affinity between Istanbul and Algiers, both cities, after all, molded by Ottoman mastery: "Building their Casbah, the Turks have created a masterpiece of architecture and urbanism."[24] Nevertheless, as Çelik points out, in spite of his admiration for all aspects of Turkish culture, Le Corbusier remains practically silent on the subject of local culture in Algeria. While lamenting the rapid change in Istanbul, notably the burning down of old buildings and rebuilding programs that were mostly in European hands, he recognized the strengths of colonial urbanism and the virtues of the *mission civilisatrice*—inextricably linked with French domination of North and West Africa. Not dissimilar to the strategies of French urbanism in Morocco, Le Corbusier's views coincided with Marshal Lyautey's notion of city planning in lieu of military force: the preservation of the medinas was a priority alongside the building of the new, European-style cities—a view translated into Le Corbusier's *plan directeur* for Algiers (fig. 5).

This dichotomous vision of Algiers may have derived, in part, from Le Corbusier's experience of Istanbul during his youthful journey across Eastern Europe. The then twenty-three-year-old artist known as Charles-Edouard Jeanneret undertook a voyage to Berlin, passing through central Europe, Turkey, Greece, and Italy before returning to Paris. Referring to it as a *voyage utile,* Jeanneret divided his itinerary into three categories rather than into topographical sections: "C" for culture, "F" for folklore, and "I" for industry. Berlin was marked with an I, central Europe with an F, and from Istanbul to Italy with a C. The letter C is also the first letter of Constantinople, which he writes about in a letter to August Klipstein, the art historian who became his traveling companion:

5 Skyscraper, marina quarter, business center, Algiers, February 1, 1939 / Wolkenkratzer, Hafenviertel, Geschäftszentrum, Algier, 1.2.1939
Watercolor on gelatine printing paper / Aquarell auf Gelatinefotopapier, 69 x 95 cm

You dream in Constantinople; I have often dreamed [of it]. But my studious life kept pushing the dome of Saint Sophia into the blue of mirages. But today circumstances have changed. I left Behrens on 1st April and have decided to finish my studies . . . in the dream. Therefore I dreamed of Rome. I'll stick with Rome, but agree to go to Constantinople. So if you want me as a companion, dream about this great enterprise in all seriousness.[25]

The notion of dream as a metonymy for near-obsession with the Orient clearly informs Le Corbusier's acquaintance and appraisal of Algiers, whose Casbah, "unspoiled by nineteenth century industrialization and taste, was a lively cluster of folk architecture. . . . All these realities, around 1930, forcefully entered the orbit of Le Corbusier's thinking."[26] Central to the "oriental dream" was his "obsession with the female form,"[27] albeit illustrated in a mythical manifestation on the cover of *Poésie*: "I believe in the *skin* of things, like that of women."[28] The figure of *La femme à la licorne* features in a number of sketches, a tapestry, and a mural from the nineteen-forties to the nineteen-sixties.[29] In his notebooks (1950–54), the architect wrote the following:

> This idea (notion) of a human bestiary may have come to me unconsciously from frequent contact [with it] across the world and across all social strata, with men and women, in business, committees, intimacy. The characters appear, describing their meanings and bringing or // putting forward // their typology.[30]

The sketches of a horned woman are mostly undated, and the female figure is horizontal rather than vertical as on the cover of *Poésie*. One dated sketch, *La femme à la licorne,* is both vertical and supported by an oversized hand.[31] Interestingly, the background is devoid of the city of Algiers; it merely features a coastline: a sign that the plan had not yet been fully realized. The title, *Garder mon aile dans ta main,* is a quotation from a poem by Mallarmé.[32] In contrast with the nudity of the female figure on the cover, the Casbah is represented by a burka-like shape complete with concealing net or grille around the eyes (plate 15), not unlike his depiction of a veiled Arab woman (fig. 6).[33] Another oversized hand holding a series of curvy, unidentified shapes[34] accompanies the text describing France being "reborn from its cinders" and the "conquering" solution of urbanism,[35] intimating the power of the architect's hand in the resolution of Algiers's problems: "Mr. Mayor, concede that this idea is not for a hundred years' time. It is for the immediate present. It ties in with the future solutions of Algiers, capital of Africa."[36]

It seems that an artist Le Corbusier respected deeply, Picasso, was equally captivated by the women of Algiers and may have sought inspiration for his *Femmes d'Alger* after seeing Le Corbusier's murals at Cap Martin.[37] Picasso's series of etchings commissioned by Ambroise Vollard were inspired by associations with the *corrida* as well as by classical mythology (epitomized by the figure of the Minotaur). Two engravings in particular call to mind Le Corbusier's horned woman: a winged

6   *Veiled Arabian Woman / Verschleierte Araberin*
Graphite pencil and black ink on paper / Grafitstift, schwarze
Tinte auf Papier, 10.5 x 16 cm

bull with a woman's breasts and a "bird woman."[38] While Picasso feminizes and therefore humanizes the bull, Le Corbusier animalizes and, in a sense, objectifies the female figure, with her curvaceous hips and bounteous breasts. If Picasso depicts the artist (himself) with the head of a Greek hero in his Vollard etchings, Le Corbusier's enlarged hand embodies the architect's artistic might. Similarly, Le Corbusier's *La femme à la licorne* is analogous to Picasso's bird-woman and winged bull—both refer obliquely to classic mythology.

The remaining illustrations of the *Poésie* can best be described as graphic collages of black ink superimposed with the occasional blotch of blue. The artist sometimes inserts a human eye, suggesting the human dimension, while an airplane gliding above the marina embodies progress (plate 11). For all it is worth, Le Corbusier's little art book reflects his visionary outlook on design—urban and artistic—albeit wrapped up in controversy. For a contemporary architect to admit, as does Jean Nouvel, that "architects are today very relative, because they're no longer taking part in the fundamental urban decision-making" says a great about Le Corbusier's era and the potential for a more holistic approach to urbanism. As Nouvel continues, "I think that from the moment you're not in the decision-making that takes into account the landscape, the colors, the relationship with the other buildings, the context, you can't really go anywhere interesting; because then each person is just doing their own little thing."[39] This description fits contemporary London perfectly: Le Corbusier's idealized urban plan for what was fundamentally an alien culture may have not been the ideal solution for Algiers, but the amount of thought and time he spent on its possible realization held the keys to something potentially revolutionary.

Notes

1   Rowan Moore, "Eileen Gray's E1027: A Lost Legend of 20th-Century Architecture is Resurrected," *The Guardian,* May 2, 2015.

2   The present translation is based on the version of Le Corbusier's text published in Rémi Baudouï, ed., *Poésie sur Alger—Histoire d'un Ouvrage* (Algiers: Éditions Barzakh, 2013). All references to the original French text are to this edition unless otherwise noted. Le Corbusier's comparison of urban blight to illness refers to Camus's novel *The Plague,* first published in 1947. Expressing his condolences to Camus's wife, Le Corbusier wrote: "Camus was a member of our band in 1931, 32, 33, in Algiers, while he was tracing a potentially heroic adventure! Alas!" Fondation Le Corbusier (FLC), Correspondence with Albert Camus.

3   The most innovative aspect of the skyscraper was the inclusion of *brise-soleil,* concrete shutters that deflected direct sunlight.

4   Of this edition, 2,525 copies were printed, 1–25 on La Fuma paper and the remaining 2,500 on Alpha paper from the Papéterie du Marais.

5   "Langues Français–Anglais," FLC 43-7 412.

6   I would like to give special thanks to Christine Mongin and Isabelle Godienau for their help at the Fondation Le Corbusier during my visit in October 2014.

7   Rainer Maria Rilke, *Lettres à un Jeune Poète,* published by Bernard Grasset (Paris, 1941).

8   Le Corbusier, "Urbanisation de la ville d'Alger, 1931–34," *Œuvre complète, 1929–34*, p. 174.

9   Quoted in Zeinep Çelik, *Urban Forms and Colonial Confrontations: Algiers under French Rule* (Berkeley, CA, and London, 1997), p. 50. On perceptions of hygiene in French colonies, see Cleo Cantone, "Senegal Rising: Emerging Anglophone Scholarship on Francophone West Africa," *Canadian*

80   POSTFACE

Journal of African Studies, 2015, http://www.tandfonline.com/doi/abs/10.1080/00083968.2014.941201.

10 Rémi Baudouï, *Poésie sur Alger* (see note 2), p. 55.

11 Unless otherwise noted, this and all other translations from the French are my own. See Le Corbusier, "Urbanisation de la ville d'Alger, 1931–34," *Œuvre complète, 1929–34,* p. 24: "L'architecture arabe nous donne un enseignement précieux. Elle s'apprécie à la marche, avec le pied; c'est en marchant, en se déplaçant, que l'on voit se développer les ordonnances de l'architecture. C'est un principe contraire à l'architecture baroque qui est conçue sur le papier, autour d'un point fixe théorique. Je préfère l'enseignement de l'architecture arabe . . . Ils ont pu se loger si nombreux et à l'aise, dans les ombres diverses de la cour, dans l'espace des horizons de la terrasse, parce que cette architecture arabe détient le secret des dimensions humaines. Ces gens, ces guerriers terribles, aimaient a se reposer bien et entendaient gouter à la joie de vivre." Le Corbusier also mentions the excellence of Arab city planning in *Looking at City Planning* (New York, 1963), p. 122.

12 Carl Jung, *Memories, Dreams, and Reflections* (London, 1995), Letter to Emma Jung, Sousse, March 15, 1920, p. 371.

13 Edward W. Said, *Power, Politics, and Culture: Interviews with Edward W. Said,* edited and with an introduction by Gauri Viswanathan (New York, 2002), p. 31.

14 Jung, *Memories* (see note 12), p. 272.

15 Le Corbusier, *Poésie* (see note 2), p. 40.

16 Jung, *Memories* (see note 12), p. 267.

17 Ibid. p. 274.

18 Le Corbusier, *Le poème de l'angle droit* (Ostfildern, 2012), p. 109.

19 Le Corbusier, *Urbanisme projets A, B, C, et H (Alger), 1930–39*: "ALGÉROIS, TA VOITURE NE PEUT PLUS CIRCULER PARCE QUE LE STATIONNEMENT ENCOMBRE TES RUES. IL FAUT DONC T'INTERDIRE DE STATIONNER, MAIS ALORS TA VOITURE

TE DEVIENT INUTILE ET INUTILES AUSSI SON VENDEUR, TON
GARAGISTE, TON RÉPARATEUR, TON MARCHAND D'ESSENCE,
TON ASSUREUR."

20 Le Corbusier, Letter to the mayor of Algiers, *Œuvre complète, 1929–34,* p. 176.

21 Alexander von Segel, "Le Cheval de Troie du Bolchevisme,"
quoted in Jean-Louis Cohen, "A Journey through 'the Modern
World,'" in *Le Corbusier's Secret Laboratory—from Painting to
Architecture*, ed. Jean-Louis Cohen and Staffan Ahrenberg,
(Ostfildern, 2013), p. 78.

22 Zeinep Çelik, "Le Corbusier, Orientalism, Colonialism,"
Assemblage 17 (1992), pp. 58–77.

23 Le Corbusier, "Le Folklore est l'expression fleurie des traditions," *Voici la France de ce mois,* June 16, 1941, p. 31, quoted
in Çelik, "Le Corbusier, Orientalism, Colonialism" (see note 21),
p. 62.

24 Le Corbusier, *Poésie* (see note 2), p. 16: "Construisant leur
Casbah (4), les Turcs avaient atteint au chef-d'oeuvre d'architecture et d'urbanisme."

25 Quoted in Marc Bérada, "La clef c'est: regarder," Introduction to Le Corbusier's *Voyage d'Orient, 1910–11* (Paris,
2011), p. 11.

26 Stanislav von Moos, *Le Corbusier—Elements of a Synthesis*
(Cambridge, MA, and London, 1979), p. 201.

27 Geneviève Hendricks, "Evocative Objects and Sinuous
Forms: Le Corbusier in the Thirties," in Cohen and Ahrenberg,
Le Corbusier's Secret Laboratory (see note 21), p. 185.

28 Le Corbusier, *Quand les cathédrales étaient blanches*
(Biarritz, 1965), p. 22.

29 A curved horn pouring money into a cuboid labeled "caisse
municipale" appears in the architect's *Œuvre complète, 1929–
34* (p. 141) as a reference to the practicality of vertical cities.
In a later sketch from 1962, the horned woman is renamed:
"The unicorn comes from the sea," AVC, Charitable Foundation,

82 POSTFACE

Moscow, gouache and pencil on paper, in Cohen and Ahrenberg, *Le Corbusier's Secret Laboratory* (see note 21), p. 235.

30 Le Corbusier, *Carnets (2) 1950–54* (Paris, 1981), n. 707:
"Cette idée (notion) de bestiaire humain m'est peut-être venue
inconsciemment du contact si fréquent et à travers tout le
monde et à travers toutes les couches sociales, avec les hommes et les femmes, dans les affaires, les comités, l'intimité. Les
caractères apparaissant, qualifiant les sens et portant ou // proposant // leur typologie."

31 See *Garder mon aile dans ta main,* 1946. Sketch in colored
pencil, ink, and pastel, 70 x 21 cm, lot 108, auctioned September 26, 2007, by Zürichsee Auktionen, http://www.artvalue.
com/auctionresult--le-corbusier-charles-edouard-j-garder-
mon-aile-dans-ta-main-1637388.htm.

32 Ô rêveuse, pour que je plonge
Au pur délice sans chemin,
Sache, par un subtil mensonge,
Garder mon aile dans ta main.
Excerpt from "Autre éventail de Mademoiselle Mallarmé," in
Stéphane Mallarmé Poems (Berkeley, CA, and Los Angeles,
1957), p. 68.

33 Le Corbusier sketched numerous nudes and semi-nudes
of Algerian women, some with their faces veiled.

34 Le Corbusier, *Poésie* (see note 2), p. 45.

35 Le Corbusier, *Poésie* (see note 2), p. 44.

36 Le Corbusier, *Œuvre complète, 1929–34,* p. 176.

37 Alan Read, *Architecturally Speaking: Practices of Art, Architecture, and the Everyday* (New York, 2000), p. 150.

38 Stephen Coppard, *Picasso Prints—The Vollard Suite* (London, 2012), plate 13, *Winged Bull Watched by Four Children,*
etching, 1934, and plate 24, *Masked Figures and Bird-Woman,*
aquatint and etching, November 1934.

39 Quoted in Amelia Stein, "Jean Nouvel: 'Architecture is still
an art, sometimes,'" *The Guardian,* May 15, 2015.

DIE POESIE ALGIERS

Le Corbusier

Max Pol Fouché hat mich aufgefordert,
für *Fontaine* zu schreiben.

Fontaine ist ein Hafen für die poetischen Schiffe eines von den Folgen einer
gewaltigen Niederlage betäubten Frankreichs – eines Frankreichs, das eines
schönen Tages in die Knie gezwungen
wurde, weil es sich die unbeschreibliche
Rohheit des ausgehenden ersten Maschi-
nenzeitalters gefallen ließ, in dem Kauf-
leute das Sagen hatten, während die An-
ständigen und die Leidenschaftlichen auf
diesem Markt nicht mehr hoch im Kurs
standen. Ein widerwärtiger Jahrmarkt,
ein Gaukelspiel, Akademismus an den
Schaltstellen (das ewig Alte, das ständig
Überholte). Das sind die Bedingungen,
unter denen unverhofft Werte wieder
zum Tragen kommen, die einem Denken,
einer Poesie, einer Lyrik, die forschen und
entdecken, gebieten, sich zum Anführer,
zum Motor zu machen, dem Vorhaben der
Erneuerung die Richtung vorzuzeichnen,
das Bemühen des Landes aus der Mittelmäßigkeit herauszuholen, die Kräfte der

Begeisterung zu wecken, das Feuer im Herzen zu entfachen, jene Gesten der Selbstlosigkeit und Uneigennützigkeit hervorzubringen, die die Würze des Lebens sind, die im Grunde die Freude selbst sind, das Strahlen, das Glück. Die Menschen aus der Trivialität herauszuheben und ihnen den Weg zur Entdeckung des Herzens zu eröffnen, wo jeder sein eigener Herr ist, frei, die Reichtümer zu ernten, die das Leben bereithält.

Dies ist ein aktueller Gesichtspunkt. Er wird sichtbar machen, welche Dinge des täglichen Gebrauchs wirklich wertvoll sind. Die Poesie, führend in Sachen Reduktion und eine Meisterin der Sozialität. Wir wissen wohl (und die heutige Zeit beweist es), dass Gefühle die elektrische Spannung einer Gesellschaft sind. Das Gefühl stellt Sie auf eine bestimmte Stufe, und von deren Höhe hängt es ab, wie man die Dinge bewertet.

Stadtplanung und Städtebau sind das Abbild der Vitalität einer Gesellschaft. Auf der ganzen Welt bestimmen unübersehbar Chaos, Leichtfertigkeit und Konfusion das Bild. Mittelmäßigkeit der Tage und der Leben, trostlose Städte, in Europa wie in Amerika. Wie lässt sich diese Misere beseitigen? Die Städte haben die Pest ...

Sie sind krank, weil die Poesie seit Ge-
nerationen aus dem Herzen der Berufe
verschwunden ist. Die Architektur und
die Architekten sind sehr tief gefallen.
Der Ingenieur – Meister, König und Usur-
pator zugleich – hat die Welt mit seinen
Erfindungen überzogen. Diese Erfindungen – die Resultate nüchterner Berechnungen, jener Berechnungen der Gesetze
der Natur – wurden in keiner Weise auf-
gewertet durch eine erhellende Eigen-
schaft: die Harmonie. Nein, sie kamen im
Gewand der Prätention daher; die ein
oder andere Architekturvorlesung hatte
die Entwürfe verpatzt. So viele Monstrosi-
täten haben Algier damals verschandelt,
genau wie sie Paris verschandelt hatten.

Dreizehn Jahre der Beharrlichkeit und
unermüdlichen Arbeit – und irgendwie
auch eine Fügung des Schicksals – haben
mich im Frühjahr 42 hierher geführt, um
den maßgeblichen Personen die Früchte
langer Überlegungen zu überbringen: einen *Masterplan* (2). Einen »Masterplan«
für Algier und seine Umgebung.

Das Wort ist neu, die Sache ist ein No-
vum. Es ist der Keim der Zukunft, den
man mitten in das bestehende Chaos in-
jiziert und der in der Lage ist, das Verhalten der Menschen zu lenken – die Freude,

die wieder Einzug im Kern der Urzelle, der Familie, gehalten hatte, und der Bürgersinn, die Synthese aus Begeisterung, Vertrauen und Überzeugung, der sich damals in den Gemeinschaftsarbeiten widerspiegelte – und der den Unternehmungen ihre unwiderstehliche Kraft und Stärke verleiht und die leuchtende Stadt über die glanzlosen Misserfolge dieser Zeit erhebt.

Poesie strahlt über Algier: ein Masterplan – der Masterplan – wird sie zum Vorschein bringen.

Sie ist keineswegs subjektiv, sondern von der Realität Nordafrikas geprägt. Von Regeln befreit stellt der Masterplan unter Beweis, dass zutiefst menschliche Quellen der Freude Platz greifen werden, wenn man die Ressourcen, die der Ort bereithält, in den Dienst der Menschen stellt (3). Freuden, die ich schon seit 15 Jahren als »unabdingbar« bezeichne – als da sind Sonne, Platz, Grün. »Unabdingbare Freuden«.

Wir befinden uns in Afrika. Diese Sonne, diese weite azurblaue Wasserfläche, dieses Grün bildeten ebenso die Kulisse

für die Gesten Salambos und die Taten
Scipios und Hannibals wie für Kheir-ed-
Din Barbarossa. Das Meer, das Atlasge-
birge und die Berge der Kabylei entfalten
ihre blaue Pracht. Die Erde ist rot. Die
Vegetation besteht aus Palmen, Eukalyp-
tusbäumen, Gummibäumen, Korkeichen,
Olivenbäumen und Feigenkakteen. Jasmin
und Mimosen verströmen ihren Duft.
Vom Vordergrund bis zu den Grenzen des
Horizonts eine einzige Sinfonie.

Mit der Kasbah (4) hatten die Türken
ein architektonisches und städtebauliches
Meisterwerk geschaffen. Doch die angrenzenden natürlichen Reichtümer sind
der europäischen Kolonialisierung der
vergangenen fünfzig Jahre zum Opfer gefallen, und die neue Stadt wurde ohne
Skrupel in eine Steinwüste verwandelt,
deren dicht gedrängte Häuser sich über
lärmende Straßen neigen. Die Bewohner
drängen sich auf den Trottoirs der Rue
d'Isly/Rue Michelet,[1] der im Grunde ein-
zigen Straße, um abends, in den schönen
Stunden, in der angenehmen Milde der
kühleren Abendluft zwischen den Fassa-
den von Mietshäusern lustlos zu prome-
nieren (5). Von den Fenstern ihrer Zim-
mer blicken sie, mit Ausnahme einiger
weniger, die dem entfliehen konnten, auf

nichts als Mauern, die von sie anstarren-
den Fenstern durchbrochen sind.

.   .   .   .

Einem Impuls folgend habe ich beschlossen, diese Quartiere zu durch-
schneiden.

Ich habe quer durch das Häusermeer
einen Schnitt gemacht und bin, der steilsten Linie der Klippe folgend über nicht
enden wollende Treppen zwischen Häusern, deren Türen in ebenso viele Unter-
wie Obergeschosse münden (Wolkenkratzer, die man ungeachtet der Bauordnung
errichtet hat) oder durch schmucke Gäss-
chen, die für den, der sich dort auskennt,
das Meer mit dem höchsten Punkt der
Berghänge verbinden geradewegs zum
Fort-L'Empereur,[2] in 250 Meter Höhe auf-
gestiegen. Eine Jakobsleiter, die den hüb-
schen Namen Lys du Pac trägt. Bei Höhen-
kote 100 überquert man den Weg, der, an
die steil aufragende Klippe geschmiegt,
um den ehemaligen türkischen Aquädukt
Telemly[3] führt. Dann, wenn man den Chemin Pouyanne erreicht, geht es erneut
bergauf, rasch, fruchtbar, reich an Beloh-
nungen. Der Horizont hat sich aufgetan,
breitet sich vor einem aus; das Blickfeld
ist unermesslich weit: Hier und da sieht

man das Meer oder Berge, die gleichsam wie Theaterkulissen von Eukalyptusbäumen oder Pinien umrahmt werden, und schwindelerregend steil aufragende Hügel. Schafe und Ziegen (6), mitunter auch Esel, grasen auf einer der auf solch zerklüfteten Böden seltenen Weiden. Nach unten gibt das Laub der umstehenden Bäume immer wieder bruchstückhafte Blicke auf Ozeandampfer frei, die sich langsam, und als sähe man sie durch ein Fernrohr, ins Blickfeld schieben und die, wenn sie Anker geworfen haben, auf die Unterzeichnung der nächsten Friedensverträge warten. Schwarze Schiffsrümpfe und weiße Aufbauten, rote Schornsteine, blaues Meer, graues Astwerk und rotbraune Erde – eine bizarre Collage, in der auf ein und derselben Leinwand Schluchten hinabstürzen, Baumkronen emporragen, Wellen heranrollen. Feigenkakteen säumen die Hütten der Eingeborenen. Da und dort, über einer Umfassungsmauer, hat die ausladende strahlenförmige Krone einer Palme die Horizontale des Meeres zum Maßstab genommen.

Es war nur ein Katzensprung bis hierher, in dieses Azurblau, in dem sich Meer und Himmel vereinen, in eine ungeahnte märchenhafte Welt, die von noch ganz in

fernen Zeiten verhafteten Kabylen be-
wohnt wurde und von Aussteigern aus
Europa, die sich dort eine Hütte oder eine
Villa gebaut hatten und die den schweiß-
treibenden täglichen Weg einen Bergpfad
hinauf angesichts dieser Grandiosität
und dieser reinen Luft nicht scheuten.

Algerier begeben sich dort nicht hin,
sind nie dorthin gegangen, würden dort
nicht hingehen und werden niemals dorthin gehen, wenn ...

.   .   .   .

Ich habe also quer durch die Stadt, in
das Dickicht der zweihundert Meter
Mietshäuser samt der diversen Straßen-
bahnen, Linien- und Reisebusse – dort,
wo sich die Menschen verbergen – einen
Schnitt gemacht. Dann habe ich noch
einmal zweihundert Meter zurückgelegt,
im Vogelflug von steilen Hängen herab,
Kanäle, Treppen erklimmend (7).

Ich befand mich auf den »Anhöhen von
Algier«, der unschätzbaren Reserve, den
Orten, an denen sich das urbane Ge-
schehen abspielen wird, der Bühne des in
Kürze zu erwartenden Schauspiels der
menschlichen Habitation, des Spiels des
möglichen Glücks einer Gesellschaft, die
das düstere Zeitalter der Dummheit und

der Scheußlichkeit, der Trägheit und des
Laisser-faire hinter sich gelassen hat, des
neuen Spiels einer Herde, die gute Hirten
gefunden hat.

Diese Steigung entlang der steilsten
Linie der Klippe bezeichne ich als eine
der vertikalen Achsen von Algier (8).

Die gesamte Klippe entlang gibt es
noch weitere solcher, ebenso hübscher
Achsen, die an die Küste geschmiegt, die
Kruste der hässlichen Gebäude durchdringen und sich allesamt zum Licht hin
öffnen ...

Diese Achse erstreckt sich bis zum
Obelisken von Fort-L'Empereur, jenem
alles überragenden weißen, sich aus al-
ten braunen Mauern erhebenden Wahr-
zeichen. Der braune Stein – zweckmäßig
und schön anzusehen – war in früherer
Zeit gebräuchlich. Schon die Römer ver-
wendeten ihn, und später kam er hier, bei
dieser Festung, zum Einsatz, die nicht,
wie man meinen könnte, von Kaiser Napoleon III. stammt, sondern von Karl V.: Die
Kasbah der Barbareskenstaaten war un-
einnehmbar. Auf der zu ihren Füßen gelegenen, kaum zweihundert Meter ent-
fernten Île de l'Amirauté ging der Kaiser
an Land und ließ Kanonen aufstellen.
Nach einem langen Umweg über die

Bucht, das Kap Matifou und die Klippe erreichte er mit weiteren Truppen diesen in zweihundert Meter Höhe gelegenen Punkt und errichtete zweihundert Meter hinter der Kasbah, in Schussweite, eine Festung, die er mit weiteren Kanonen ausstattete.

Länge und Höhe sind gleich und betragen jeweils zweihundert Meter. Dies wiederholt sich merkwürdigerweise, nimmt man die Dicke und den Umfang zusammen, die ausreichen, um die Wege zum Glück verborgen zu halten.

In zweihundert Meter Entfernung befinden sich die herrlichen Bezirke, die die Bewohner, würden sie sich dorthin begeben, glücklich machen würden! Doch sie gehen nicht dorthin. Sie sind eingepfercht in den Käfigen (9) der Mietshäuser, wo die Luft schlecht ist und von wo aus man nichts, rein gar nichts sieht: weder das Meer noch die Schiffe, weder die Berge noch die weiten Ebenen, weder Bäume noch die rote Erde und auch niemanden, der es versteht, es sich gut gehen zu lassen.

Ein allseits bekannter Bürgermeister, mit dem ich – es muss so um das Jahr 1930 gewesen sein – darüber sprach, erklärte mir, als ich ihm voller Begeisterung von meiner Entdeckung berichtete und vorschlug, dort oben dreihunderttausend Menschen anzusiedeln: »Gewiss, gewiss, ... ich bin schon einmal dort vorbeigekommen, am Fort-L'Empereur, als ich in der Kaserne stationiert war, vor vierzig Jahren ...« Und just in Algier und just in den städtischen Gremien und just als dieses Gespräch stattfand, plante man den Bau *einer Metro, unter der Erde*, um die Bevölkerung auf dem schnellsten Weg in weit entfernte Siedlungen zu befördern – dorthin, wo sich Fuchs und Hase Gute Nacht sagen! Außerdem arbeitete man (10) an Plänen für Mietskasernen am Fuße der Kasbah, auf dem Gelände »der Marina«, das durch den Abriss von Elendsbehausungen frei geworden war. Auf dem Körper von Französisch-Afrika und mitten im Gesicht von Algier, mitten auf der Nase dieses Gesichtes, jawohl: Mietskasernen! Auf diesem ganz besonderen Fleckchen Afrikas!!! Malheur! Gedankenlosigkeit! Ignoranz! Vernichtung der poetischen Werte! Ein Mordanschlag auf die Poeten!

In diesen tief gelegenen Stadtbezirken, am Rand der Wellen, in diesem Hafen mit all den Erdwällen und dem Schotter, wo überall das Salzwasser eindringt, würden sich Palmen, die hohen Palmen der Oasen, wohlfühlen. Als Wald, als Palmenhain, sich sanft in der Meeresbrise wiegend, würden sie den gesamten Hafen bedecken. Man müsste sie nur an den unzähligen »toten Punkten«, jenen Plätzen, die nicht von Transportanlagen, von Fässern, Ballen und Kisten, von Kohle und Erzen besetzt sind, pflanzen. Auf dem Boden nimmt eine Palme nicht mehr Platz ein als ein Schemel; in einer Höhe von zwanzig Metern entfaltet sie sich wie ein Feuerwerk. Der Hafen von Algier befindet sich unterhalb der weitläufigen Gewölbestrukturen, auf denen das große Plateau mit dem Boulevard und den Arkaden ruht. Der moderne Hafen ist heute nicht mehr als eine Aussparung im Wasser auf dem Plan der Ingenieure: Zwischen Bergen von afrikanischen Feld- und Gartenfrüchten, zwischen Schwergütern, Kohle und Erzen herrscht ein reges Treiben. Fülle und zugleich Mittelmaß der Handelsgeschäfte, der Geldgeschäfte. Zwischen dem Kheir-ed-Din-Pier (11) und dem Bug der Bastion 15 im Dock von Agha – auf einer Länge von tausend Metern – wiegt sich eine einzige einsame Palme, ein alter Weiser oder ein alter Narr mit einer prächtigen Krone, aus einem Zufall geboren. Sie allein reicht aus, um den Poeten

in einem zu wecken, um einem eine Idee
einzugeben, um einen zu ermuntern, den
ersten Schritt zu tun. Einsam im Hafen
von Algier ist sie schon für sich genommen Genius, Verheißung, Strahlen und
Freude über den Hafen. Sie beherrscht
die Gedanken ...

Herr Präfekt, ein Brief von Ihnen, an
die Herren Ingenieure des Straßenbau-
amts von Algier gerichtet, mit dem Sie sie
anweisen, an jedem »toten Punkt« zwischen den Verkehrsadern und den Hafen-
speichern Dattelkerne einzupflanzen,
und Ihnen ist die ehrenvollste Belohnung
gewiss. In zwanzig Jahren wird man
sagen: »die Palmen des Präfekten von
Algier«. Sie werden den ganzen Hafen
überziehen, sie werden die Sicht auf die
Molen und Hafenbecken,[4] auf die Fracht-
und Passagierschiffe, auf Kriegsschiffe
und Schlepper, auf die weißen Segel der
Jachten umrahmen und werden neben
dem Auf und Ab der blauen Wellen einen
sanft wogenden grünen Teppich zu Füßen
der Stadt ausbreiten. An windigen Tagen
die weißen Schaumkronen des Mittel-
meers und das Rauschen der Palmen.

Hebe- und Fördergeräte werden zwischen ihnen hindurchfahren; der Plun-
der und das Sammelsurium der ge- und

entladenden Waren werden dann nur
noch ein zweitrangiges visuelles Erlebnis
sein ...

Kommen wir zum Kern der Algierfrage.
Wir hatten bereits darüber gesprochen,
dreihunderttausend Bewohner auf den
Anhöhen anzusiedeln und am Fuße der
Stadt überall Palmen zu pflanzen (12).

Das buchtenreiche Algier liegt auf
dem Meridian von Paris – El Golea – Gao,
dem Meer, dem französischen Mutterland, Europa vis-à-vis, ein schmaler, lang
gestreckter Küstenstreifen, der dennoch
ausreicht, um die faszinierenden, brillan-
ten, vollendeten architektonischen Züge
der künftigen französischen Hauptstadt
Afrikas erahnen zu lassen. Vom Meer aus
werden die Schiffe sie schon von weitem
auftauchen sehen (13).

Für sich betrachtet ist Algier mit seiner sichelförmigen Reede *eine Stadt, die
sich selbst ansieht* (14). Es ist der Mühe
wert, hier architektonische Meisterwerke
zu errichten: Noblesse oblige!

Werden nun aber im Gegenteil ein-
seitig partikularistische Sichtweisen und

Manipulationen dazu führen, dass diese
Vorsehung im Keim erstickt wird, obwohl
sie in der Geschichte, der Geografie, der
Topografie festgeschrieben ist? Ist das
»Marina«-Viertel bedroht? Wird das Kap
von Algier, dieses afrikanische, auf dem
Meridian von Paris gelegene Kap zu einem
städtebaulichen Fehltritt werden (15)?

Als erfahrener Pilger in diesem poten-
ziellen Wunderland, der von einem Glauben erfüllt ist, an dem er 13 Jahre, die er
darauf verwendete, ihr städtebauliches
Potenzial herauszuarbeiten, unbeirrbar
festgehalten hat, habe ich beim Gouverneur, beim Präfekten, beim Bürgermeister
vorgesprochen, habe ich mich an jeden
einzelnen dieser höchsten Verwaltungs-
instanzen einer Stadt, einer Region, Afrikas mit den Worten gewendet:

Herr Gouverneur, Herr Präfekt, Herr
Bürgermeister, Poesie liegt über diesem
Ort, der sich Algier nennt, auf afrikani-
schem Boden, der einst nacheinander
drei große Zivilisationen beheimatete:
die der Phönizier, die der Römer, die der
Muslime. Spuren, Zeugnisse, die überall
zu finden sind, warnen uns vor der Mittelmäßigkeit unserer ökonomischen Unternehmungen; sie sind ein Beweis dafür,
dass es stets möglich ist, etwas Großes zu

erreichen, vorausgesetzt es herrscht Einhelligkeit im Denken.

Mit der ersten unheilvollen Epoche der »civilisation machiniste« wurde ein neues Kapitel aufgeschlagen; die zweite wird Feuer, Blut, Unglück nach sich ziehen – die Epoche der Harmonie. Ein Gedanke kann die Fäden unserer über Zeit und Raum verteilten Taten zusammenführen, in der Gewissheit, sie zu einer Einheit zusammenzufügen.

Das Spiel wird auf der ganzen Welt gespielt. Es sind nicht die Götter des Olymp, die von ihrem Wohnsitz herabsteigen werden, um bei uns Taten zu vollbringen, die die Menschen vermeintlich zu vollbringen nicht imstande sind. Es sind Menschen wie Sie, die ihre Namen, ihr Andenken, ihre Taten aufgrund der Qualität der Initiativen, die sie ergreifen, und der Verantwortung, die sie übernehmen, zum Olymp führen werden (16). Es liegt in Ihren Händen: das Schicksal der fünfhunderttausend Einwohner des heutigen und des zukünftigen Algier; der Glanz dieses afrikanischen Frankreich, dessen Kopf – die Hauptstadt – sich auf Ihr Geheiß in ein Juwel verwandeln wird; die Anerkennung des Mutterlandes, weil Sie in einem Augenblick gehandelt haben, in

dem andere sich damit begnügt hätten,
die laufenden Geschäfte zu erledigen;
das Staunen der Welt angesichts dieses
Phönix Frankreichs, der ein weiteres Mal,
und in einem ganz und gar erbarmungs-
würdigen Zustand, aus seiner Asche auf-
steigt ...

Ein zweihundert Meter großes Dickicht
von Häusermauern, das es mit Ihren Gedanken zu durchdringen gilt, und eine
Höhe von zweihundert Metern, die es mithilfe einer stadtplanerischen Lösung zu
erobern gilt. An diesem Meeresstrand
einen Ton – ein Potenzial, das in diesem
Fleckchen Erde schlummert – zu kneten
und ihm dabei Glanz zu verleihen, und zu
verbieten – und zwar ein für allemal und
auf der Stelle –, dass er für billige Ar-
beiten in Dummheit und Verirrung er-
starrt!

Die Poesie, die, Herr Gouverneur, Herr
Präfekt, Herr Bürgermeister, im Grunde
die wichtigste Nahrung der Menschen
ist, die Widerstandskraft verleiht, die den
Mut aufrechterhält, die den Glauben
stärkt, diese Poesie liegt über Algier, bereit, Einzug zu halten und in städtebaulichen und architektonischen Fakten Gestalt anzunehmen. Übernehmen Sie das
Ruder. Noch ist Zeit. Besprechen Sie sich

miteinander, tun sie sich zusammen, tun
sie es!

Das Urteil wird hart sein eines Tages,
wenn nichts Effektives unternommen wird,
denn man wird wissen, dass die Ange-
legenheit beizeiten verhandelt wurde.

Algier, Mai 1942

EPILOGUE

PRÄFEKT – Haben Sie den Mann erkannt, der gerade mein Büro verlassen hat?

L.-C. – Ja, das war der Herr Bürgermeister.

PRÄFEKT – Er war hier, um Ihre Verhaftung zu verlangen.

> In seiner Sitzung vom 12. Juni 1942 stimmte der Stadtrat einstimmig gegen Le Corbusiers Masterplan.

»Poésie sur Alger« konnte nicht in *Fontaine* erscheinen. Doch der Text und die Gedanken, die dahinterstehen, fanden ihre

Zustimmung, ihr Papier, ihre Typografien, ihre Plattform und ihre Förderer. Die Deutschen besetzten Algier ebenso wie Paris ... Die Leute, die diese sechs Spalten auf der ersten und der letzten Seite einer renommierten Fachzeitung veröffentlichten, übernahmen die Verantwortung für die mögliche Ausschaltung eines Gegners, der stets ausschließlich auf dem professionellen Terrain der Architektur und der Stadtplanung gekämpft hatte.

Von 1930 bis 1942 hatte er der Stadt Algier SIEBENMAL kostenlos Pläne für die Stadtgestaltung vorgelegt. Damit hat er die Stadt und ihre Behörden aus ihrer Lethargie gerissen. Ab 1936 fungierte er (ehrenamtlich) als offizieller Vertreter der französischen Regierung bei der Planungskommission für die Region Algier.

1941 schickte ihm Emery[5] eine dringliche Nachricht aus Algier, mit der er ihn vorwarnte, dass man den Plan torpedieren werde. Nachdem er der Präfektur (wiederum gratis) seinen siebten Plan vorgelegt hatte, begab er sich 1942 an Ort und Stelle, um nachzusehen und das Schweigen zu brechen. . . . .
. . . .

ENDE

Anmerkungen der Übersetzerin

1   Die Rue d'Isly heißt heute Rue Ben Mehidi Larbi und wird in den *Guides Bleus Algérie Tunisie* (Paris 1955, S. 58) als belebte Geschäftsstraße beschrieben, in der sich unter anderem der neomaurische Bon Marché (1914) befindet. Die Rue Michelet (heute Rue Didouche Mourad), die in die Rue Péguy mündete, schließt an die Rue Ben Mehidi Larbi an; vgl. *Guides Bleus Algérie Tunisie,* Paris 1986, S. 75.

2   Fort-L'Empreur trägt heute den Namen Bourdj Moulay Hassan Pacha. Vgl. *Guides Bleus Algérie Tunisie,* Paris 1974, S. 147.

3   An der Stelle des Aquädukts befindet sich heute der Boulevard Télemly, der dem Verlauf der ehemaligen ottomanischen Wasserrohre folgt. Diese wurden später restauriert; *Guides Bleus* 1955 (wie Anm. 1), S. 80.

4   Als »darse« oder »darce« (italienisch darsena) bezeichnet man, insbesondere in den Mittelmeerländern, das Hafenbecken oder Dock eines Hafens; vgl. *Larousse Illustré,* Paris 1931.

5   Pierre-André Emery war »ein weiterer, in Algerien ansässiger Architekt aus der Schule von Le Corbusier«, in: Zeynep Çelik, *Urban Forms and Colonial Confrontations: Algiers under French Rule,* Berkeley und London 1997, S. 157.

NACHWORT
Le Corbusier und
die Faszination Afrikas

Cleo Cantone, 2015

In jüngster Zeit sind die nicht unumstrittenen politischen Präferenzen Le Corbusiers neuerlich in den Fokus des Interesses gerückt. So bezichtigt der Autor Xavier de Jarcy den Architekten in einem 2015 erschienenen Buch, er habe seine Theorien in »eindeutig antidemokratischen« Magazinen propagiert. In einem ziemlich frauenfeindlichen Akt soll der Künstler Le Corbusier außerdem das moderne Haus von Eileen Gray an der Côte d'Azur mit einer »Reihe hässlicher, schreiend bunter Wandgemälde, die er vollkommen nackt malte, ›vergewaltigt‹« haben.[1] Nicht minder vernichtend sind Kritiken vonseiten der Wissenschaft an seiner Darstellung der französischen Suprematismusdebatte, mit der er sich zum Verfechter der Kolonialisierung, insbesondere des afrikanischen Kontinents, machte. Derartige Kritiken, so der Kurator einer großen Retrospektive des Centre Pompidou anlässlich des 50. Todestages von Le Corbusier, zielten darauf ab, den Künstler zu diskreditieren. All dem zum Trotz steht außer Frage, dass Le Corbusier zu den führenden Designern des 20. Jahrhunderts zählt. Auf der ganzen Welt werden seine Werke ausgestellt

oder – wie der vorliegende Band – neu aufgelegt, und es ist eine Vielzahl von Publikationen
über ihn erschienen. Der Kult der Moderne ist
noch lange nicht vorbei.

Als »livre d'art« ist Le Corbusiers *Poésie sur
Alger* Ausdruck einer Vision, eines Traums, in
dem die Stadtplanung zugleich für die »Heilung«
einer verfehlten Stadtgestaltung und einen äs-
thetischen Imperativ steht (»Die Städte haben
die Pest«).[2] Nach Belegen für den »Mangel an
Poesie«, den Le Corbusier so überzeugend
schildert, muss man in den Metropolen der
Welt nicht lange suchen: Die willkürliche Errichtung von Wolkenkratzern, der Abriss denkmal-
geschützter Bauwerke und die Beschneidung
von Grünflächen – all dies trägt zur berechtig-
ten Empörung des Architekten bei und lässt
seine – wenn auch durchaus nicht unumstrittenen – Lösungen umso plausibler erscheinen. Tatsächlich könnte man den Brief, den Le
Corbusier an den Präfekten von Algier schrieb,
ebenso gut an den Bürgermeister von London
richten. Ähnlich wie seine Zeitgenossen und
Landsmänner wollte Le Corbusier die beste-
henden lokalen Gebäudestrukturen erhalten
und in einem angrenzenden Viertel moderne
Geschäfts- und Wohnquartiere – zugegebener-
maßen in Form von Hochhäusern – errichten.
Deshalb sollte beispielsweise der höchste Wolkenkratzer, den er für Algier plante (Tafel 16),

die Moschee nicht vollständig verdecken, sondern als imposante Kulisse fungieren (Abb. 1).[3]

Nach Veröffentlichung der Erstausgabe, die 1950 bei Falaise erschien,[4] wurde *Poésie sur Alger* zweimal neu aufgelegt: 1989 von den Editions Connivences und 2013 von dem algerischen Verlag Éditions Barzakh. Die vorliegende Ausgabe trägt in gewisser Hinsicht dem Wunsch Le Corbusiers Rechnung, die »Poesie« auch in englischer Sprache zu veröffentlichen.[5] Darüber hinaus steht dahinter aber auch mein Wunsch, die eigene Neugier zu befriedigen und zu ergründen, was diesen so außerordentlich produktiven Renaissancemenschen dazu veranlasste, aus einem Stadtplanungsprojekt, das niemals realisiert wurde, ein kleinformatiges, poetisches Kunstbuch zu machen.[6] Wie aus Le Corbusiers akribisch geführten Aufzeichnungen hervorgeht, sollte das Buch – seine kleinste Publikation – das gleiche Format haben »wie Rilke 11/17 cm«.[7] Auf dem Schutzumschlag der Ausgabe von 1989 wird das Buch als ironische und emotionale Reflexion über das Algier-Projekt beschrieben, das er dreizehn Jahre lang vergebens mit großer Beharrlichkeit verfolgte. Was seine Fantasie und Kreativität bei diesem auch als »anachronistisch und abwegig« beschriebenen Projekt angeregt zu haben scheint, war nicht allein die Sanierung der Stadt, sondern vielmehr die idealistische Vorstellung von Algier als Inbegriff des künftigen »islamischen Pols«, der das Gleichgewicht der mediterranen Kulturen neu ordnen würde. Auf der Umschlagrückseite des Buches war das vierseitige Schema grafisch so dargestellt:

$$\begin{array}{ccc} & P & \\ B & & R \\ & A & \end{array}$$

Paris, Rom, Algier, Barcelona. In einem Schreiben an Brunnel, dem Bürgermeister von Algier, erläuterte Le Corbusier, seine Pole verbänden den Ärmelkanal mit dem Mittelmeer und Europa mit Afrika: »Algier wird nicht länger eine Kolonialstadt sein« und »zum Kopf Afrikas werden. Zu seiner Hauptstadt.«[8]

Mit Unterstützung des Innenministers Marcel Peyrouton empfahl sich Le Corbusier als Top-Stadtplaner, der beabsichtige, seine Theorien zur Stadtplanung auf Algier anzuwenden. Vor ihm hatten jedoch bereits drei andere Stadtplaner – René Danger, Henri Prost und Maurice Rotival – einen Masterplan präsentiert. René Lespès zufolge war das Marinaviertel mit seinen überfüllten, baufälligen, vorwiegend von Immigranten bewohnten Häusern »weder maurisch noch gänzlich europäisch« und bedurfte aufgrund der schlechten hygienischen Zustände einer Sanierung.[9]

Abgesehen vom stadtplanerischen Aspekt zeigt *Poésie sur Alger* eine intime Seite von Le Corbusiers Persönlichkeit, in Form eines poetischen Abschiedsgrußes an eine Stadt, für die er eine große Liebe hegte. Begonnen hat diese Liebesgeschichte mit der ersten Nordafrikareise, die er 1931 unternahm, dem Jahr, in dem »Französisch«-Algerien seinen 100. Jahrestag feierte. Aus diesem Anlass sollte er auf Einladung der Gesellschaft der Freunde Algeriens im März zwei Vorträge zum Thema »Die Architekturrevolution« und »Die strahlende Stadt« halten.[10] Auch wenn diesen Themen sein besonderes Interesse galt, war er nicht minder fasziniert von der islamischen Architektur:

»Die arabische Architektur lehrt uns etwas sehr Wertvolles. Sie erschließt sich im Gehen, zu Fuß. Beim Gehen, während man sich fortbewegt, erkennt man, wie sich die architektonische Struktur entfaltet. Es ist ein Prinzip, das im Gegensatz zur Barockarchitektur steht, die auf dem Papier, um einen theoretischen Fixpunkt herum, geplant wurde. Ich gebe der Lektion der arabischen Architektur den Vorzug ... Sie haben es verstanden, in so großer Zahl und dabei so komfortabel zusammenzuwohnen, an den schattigen Plätzen des Hofes, im Raum des Terrassenhorizonts, weil diese arabische Architektur das Geheimnis der menschlichen Dimensionen bewahrt. Diese Menschen, diese furchterregenden Krieger liebten es, sich auf angenehme Weise zu entspannen, und sie verstanden es, die Lebensfreude auszukosten.«[11]

1920 bereiste Carl Gustav Jung, ein Alters-
genosse Le Corbusiers, gemeinsam mit einem
Freund Algerien und Tunesien:

»Dieses Afrika ist unerhört! [...] Die arabische Stadt
ist Antike und maurisches Mittelalter, Granada und die
Märchen von Bagdad. Man denkt nicht mehr an sich,
sondern ist aufgelöst in dieses nicht zu beurteilende,
noch weniger zu beschreibende Vielerlei: in der Mauer
eine römische Säule, eine alte Jüdin von unsäglicher
Häßlichkeit in weißen Pluderhosen geht vorbei, ein
Ausrufer drängt sich mit einer Last Burnusse durch die
Menge und schreit in Kehllauten, die aus dem Kanton
Zürich stammen könnten, ein Stück tiefblauen Him-
mels, eine schneeweiße Moscheekuppel, ein Schuh-
macher näht eifrig die Schuhe in einer kleinen gewölb-
ten Nische, auf der Matte vor ihm ein heißer, blendender
Sonnenfleck [...]. Das ist alles nur elendes Gestammel,
ich weiß nicht, was Afrika mir eigentlich sagt, aber es
spricht.«[12]

Beide Autoren sprechen von der »arabischen« Stadt und der »arabischen« Architektur,
doch keiner von beiden scheint sich der Unge-
nauigkeit dieses Begriffs bewusst gewesen zu
sein. Denn in den Adern der Nordafrikaner
kann das Blut verschiedener arabischer Stäm-
me fließen. Das verbindende Element ist also
zweifellos eher der Islam, während das arabische Element kaum mehr als eine ethnische
Komponente ist. Darüber hinaus ließe sich das
Wort auch durch orientalisch ersetzen, ein Be-

griff, den Edward Said als »eine Sprache, deren Präsenz in den Institutionen und den Wissenschaften den Orientalen als Menschen eliminierte, verdrängte und durch den Typus des orientalisierten Orients ersetzte«,[13] definiert. Während Jungs Interesse vor allem dem Verhalten der Menschen galt, erfreute sich Le Corbusier an der gebauten, urbanen Umgebung: Beide Beschreibungen reihen sich in jene zeitgenössischen Tableaus ein, die ein orientalistisches Bild »des Arabers« zeichneten, der, obwohl er nach außen eine kriegerische Attitüde an den Tag legt (»diese furchterregenden Krieger«), die einer gewissen Kindlichkeit und Irrationalität nicht entbehrt, fähig ist, auf seine Weise ein zivilisiertes Leben zu führen:

»Meine Begegnung mit der arabischen Kultur hat mich offenbar überwältigend getroffen. Das emotionale, lebensnähere Wesen dieser aus Affekten lebenden, nicht reflektierenden Menschen hat einen starken suggestiven Effekt auf jene historischen Schichten in uns, die wir eben überwunden haben, oder wenigstens überwunden zu haben glauben. Es ist wie das Kindheitsparadies, dem man sich entronnen wähnt, das uns aber bei der leisesten Provokation wiederum Niederlagen beibringt. Ja, unsere Fortschrittsgläubigkeit steht in Gefahr, sich umso kindischeren Zukunftsträumen hinzugeben, je stärker unser Bewußtsein von der Vergangenheit wegdrängt. [...] Seine beinahe schwarze Hautfarbe charakterisiert [den Araber] als ›Schatten‹, aber nicht als persönlichen, sondern vielmehr als ethnischen, der nichts mit meiner bewußten Person, sondern mehr mit dem Ganzen meiner Persönlichkeit, d.h. meinem Selbst, zu tun hat. Als Herr der Kasba ist er sozusagen eine Art Schatten des Selbst // ›meines europäischen Bewusstseins‹«.[14]

Im Unterschied zu Le Corbusier, der in *Poésie sur Alger* das Zusammenfließen dreier Zivilisationen (Phönizier, Römer und Muslime) beschreibt,[15] riecht Jung den Blutgeruch in einem Boden, der »schon mit drei Zivilisationen fertig geworden ist, der panischen, der römischen und der christlichen«.[16] Während Jungs Nordafrikabild durch eine im Traum erlebte Begegnung mit einem Marabut und den Besuch einer fiktiven Medina gefiltert wird, vermittelt Le Corbusier seine Sicht in einfachen, in der französischen Ausgabe von *Poésie sur Alger* reproduzierten Skizzen. Der Faszination, die die algerische Landschaft und insbesondere ihre Architektur auf Le Corbusier ausübte, lag ohne Zweifel das zugrunde, was Jung als »eine Kindheitserinnerung« beschreibt, die »sich plötzlich mit derart lebhaftem Affekt des Bewusstseins bemächtigen kann, daß man sich wieder ganz in die ursprüngliche Situation zurückversetzt fühlt, so weckt diese anscheinend ganz andere und fremde arabische Umwelt eine Urerinnerung an eine nur zu bekannte Vorzeit, die wir anscheinend gänzlich vergessen haben«.[17] Und tatsächlich evoziert Le Corbusiers Darstellung der mythologischen Frau mit Horn auf der Stirn *(La femme à la licorne),* die auf dem Cover von *Poésie sur Alger* schwebt und die er zuvor bereits in seinem *Gedicht vom rechten Winkel* (Abb. 2)[18] verwendet hatte, diese archetypische Erinnerung.

Dass beide Autoren Bewunderung für die arabische (das heißt für die muslimische) Kultur hegen, ist unverkennbar, impliziert jedoch gleichzeitig, dass sich der indigene Araber nach wie vor als Transportmittel nur seiner Füße bedienen darf und dass als Wohnort für ihn ausschließlich die Medina infrage kommt. Die Verwandlung Algiers in eine radikal moderne Musterstadt war in Wirklichkeit alles andere als radikal, sondern hatte im Gegenteil die Erhaltung der »bezaubernden«, unveränderlichen »traditionellen« indigenen Viertel zum Ziel. Vollkommen umgestaltet werden sollte lediglich das europäische Geschäftsviertel. Sehr anschaulich führt dies – nicht zuletzt durch die Verwendung von Großbuchstaben – der folgende Text vor Augen:

»BEWOHNER VON ALGIER, DEIN AUTO KANN NICHT MEHR FAHREN, WEIL DEINE STRASSEN ZUGEPARKT SIND. ALSO MUSS MAN DIR DAS PARKEN UNTERSAGEN, DOCH DANN WIRD DEIN AUTO NUTZLOS FÜR DICH UND ÜBERLÜSSIG WERDEN AUCH SEIN VERKÄUFER, DER INHABER DEINER REPARATURWERKSTATT, DEIN AUTOMECHANIKER, DER BESITZER DEINER TANKSTELLE, DEIN VERSICHERUNGSAGENT.«[19]

Die Erhaltung der »herrlichen«, »authentischen« Medina – »die man umgestalten kann, aber nie, nie zerstören darf!«[20] – diente einerseits der vom Mutterland angestrebten Förderung der Tourismusindustrie. Andererseits diente sie als Rechtfertigung für die Eindämmung der Übervölkerung. Zu diesem Zweck schlug Le Corbusier vor, einige Wohnhäuser zur »Wiederbelebung« des heimischen Kunsthandwerks in kunsthandwerkliche Zentren umzuwandeln, was wiederum deren kommerziellen Wert erhöhen würde. Die Elendsviertel sollten abgerissen werden, um Parks und öffentlichen Gärten Platz zu machen. Das Straßennetz sollte hingegen als Verbindung der auf einer Anhöhe gelegenen Kasbah mit dem Marinaviertel und dem Hafen erhalten bleiben. Darüber hinaus erwog Le Corbusier, den historisch gewachsenen Teil der Stadt von der europäischen Stadt zu trennen. indem er die Medina mit einer zeitlosen Kapsel umgab, die für das Alte, das Traditionelle, für die Stagnation stehen und einen starken Kontrast zur neuen, modernen und fortschrittlichen europäischen City bilden sollte. Als Bindeglied zwischen den beiden Teilen sollte ein »Geschäfts- und Stadtzentrum« fungieren (Abb. 3).

Obwohl dies nicht ausdrücklich erwähnt wird, wäre die Rassentrennung in Le Corbusiers Vision für die »capitale française d'Afrique« nicht gänzlich aufgehoben. Dies veranschaulicht die Tafel, auf der die an der Spitze der Bucht von Algier gelegene, an die Kasbah angrenzende und als »musulman« gekennzeichnete Moschee zu sehen ist (Tafel 12, 14). Gemäß der Charta von Athen aus dem Jahr 1942 sollte die »ideale« Stadt in funktionale Einheiten gegliedert sein, und die Menschen sollten in großzügig angelegten Wohnblocks leben, die die Kritiker Le Corbusiers bestenfalls als »Gebäude auf einem Parkplatz« und schlimmstenfalls als »trojanisches Pferd des Bolschewismus« brandmarkten.[21]

Auf den Entwürfen des »plan directeur« von 1938 bildet das zwischen der Kasbah und dem Meer gelegene Marinaviertel mit seinen keilförmigen Wolkenkratzern die Grenze zum zukünftigen Geschäftszentrum (»cité d'affaires«) und den muslimischen Institutionen. Die »Betonstadt« ist also klar von der »weißen Stadt« abgegrenzt (Abb. 4). In einem geistreichen Artikel hat sich Zeynep Çelik mit Le Corbusiers noch kaum erforschter »Schwärmerei für die islamische Kultur« im Kontext des »›Orient‹-Diskurses im Frankreich des 19. Jahrhunderts und der Auseinandersetzung der Pariser Avantgarde mit der nichtwestlichen Welt in den 1920er- und 1930er-Jahren« beschäftigt.[22] Darin geht er sogar so weit, Le Corbusiers Reisebericht über Istanbul als Sicht eines Durchschnittsreisenden zu bezeichnen, die auf die zahlreichen Besucher im Laufe der Jahrhunderte rekurriert. Und er fügt kryptisch hinzu: »er wusste, was er sehen wollte«. Auf den Orientalisten Théophile Gautier beispielsweise wirkte Algier, als er sich der Stadt vom Meer her näherte, wie ein »weißlicher Schemen«. In eine ähnliche Richtung geht Le Corbusiers Feststellung, »der Kasbah von Algier [...] verdankt die gleißende Erscheinung, die die im Morgengrauen in den Hafen einlaufenden Boote willkommen heißt, den Namen Algier, die Weiße. Sie ist in diesen Ort eingemeißelt und damit ist sie ein Faktum. Sie ist im Einklang mit der Natur.«[23]

In seiner Schilderung von Istanbul stellt Le Corbusier insbesondere die »kubischen, von Kuppeln überspannten steinernen Massen« heraus und kommt zu dem Schluss, dass »große Architektur kubisch ist«. An späterer Stelle entdeckt er sogar eine Ähnlichkeit zwischen Istanbul und Algier, die letzten Endes beide von der Meisterschaft der Osmanen geprägt wurden. »Mit ihrer Kasbah hatten die Türken ein architektonisches und städtebauliches Meisterwerk geschaffen.«[24] Obwohl er, wie Çelik bemerkt, voller Bewunderung auf jeden Aspekt der türkischen Kultur eingeht, sagt er zur algerischen Kultur so gut wie nichts. Und während er einerseits die rasante Veränderung Istanbuls, insbesondere das Niederbrennen alter Bauwerke und die Neubauprojekte, bei denen zumeist Europäer federführend waren, beklagt, preist er andererseits die Vorzüge der kolonialen Stadtplanung und der »mission civilisatrice« –, die untrennbar mit der französischen Vorherrschaft in Nord- und Westafrika verbunden waren. Le Corbusiers Ansichten waren den Strategien der französischen Stadtplanung in Marokko nicht unähnlich und deckten sich mit der Vorstellung Marschall Lyauteys, für den die Stadtplanung eine Alternative zum Einsatz militärischer Mittel darstellte: Vorrangiges Ziel war neben der Errichtung neuer Städte im europäischen Stil die Erhaltung der Medina – eine Auffassung, die ihren Niederschlag in Le Corbusiers »plan directeur« für Algier (Abb. 5) fand.

Dieser dichotomistischen Vision von Algier mögen, wenigstens zum Teil, die Eindrücke zugrunde gelegen haben, die Le Corbusier in jungen Jahren auf seiner Osteuropareise in Istanbul sammelte. Diese Reise führte den damals 23-jährigen Künstler Charles-Edouard Jeanneret – wie Le Corbusier eigentlich heißt – über Mitteleuropa, die Türkei, Griechenland und Italien nach Berlin und von dort zurück nach Paris. Die Route dieser von ihm selbst als »voyage utile« bezeichneten Reise teilte Jeanneret in drei Kategorien ein, wobei topografische Kriterien eine eher untergeordnete Rolle spielten. Dabei stand C für »culture«, F für »folklore« und I für »industrie«. Berlin kennzeichnete er mit I,

Mitteleuropa mit F und den Abschnitt von Istanbul bis Italien mit C. Mit C beginnt im Französischen auch der Name Constantinople, der Stadt, über die er in einem Brief an den Kunsthistoriker und seinen späteren Reisebegleiter August Klipstein schrieb:

»Man träumt in Konstantinopel; ich habe oft [davon] geträumt. Doch mein arbeitsreiches Leben rückte die Kuppel von St. Sophia immer wieder in weite Ferne. Inzwischen hat sich die Situation allerdings verändert. Am 1. April habe ich bei Behrens aufgehört und habe beschlossen, meine Studien zu Ende zu führen ... im Traum. Deshalb habe ich von Rom geträumt. An Rom werde ich zwar festhalten, bin aber auch bereit, mit nach Konstantinopel zu gehen. Wenn Sie mich also als Begleiter haben möchten, träumen Sie ganz im Ernst von diesem großartigen Unterfangen.«[25]

Der Traum als Metonymie für das, was man fast schon als Orientobsession bezeichnen könnte, war unbestreitbar prägend für Le Corbusiers Begegnung mit Algier und für seine Sicht auf die Stadt, deren Kasbah, »an der weder die Industrialisierung noch der Geschmack des 19. Jahrhunderts ihre Spuren hinterlassen haben, [...] ein buntes Gemisch volkstümlicher Architektur [war]. [...] All diese Fakten drängten sich um 1930 mit Macht in die Gedankensphäre Le Corbusiers.«[26] Eine wesentliche Rolle in diesem »orientalischen Traum« spielte seine

»Begeisterung für die weibliche Gestalt«,[27] wie sie uns, wenn auch in mythischer Form, auf dem Umschlag von *Poésie sur Alger* begegnet: »Ich glaube, die Dinge haben eine *Haut,* die der von Frauen ähnlich ist.«[28] Die Figur der *Femme à la licorne (Frau als Einhorn)* taucht in einer Reihe von Skizzen, in einem Gobelin und einem Wandgemälde auf, die zwischen den 1940er- und den 1960er-Jahren entstanden.[29] In seinen *Carnets* (1950–1954) bemerkte der Architekt dazu:

> »Auf diese Idee (Vorstellung) zu einem menschlichen Bestiarium bin ich möglicherweise unbewusst durch die Männer und Frauen aus aller Herren Länder und allen sozialen Schichten gekommen, mit denen ich geschäftlich, in Komitees und privat so häufig Kontakt hatte. Die Charaktere treten zutage, determinieren die Bedeutungen und bringen ihre Typologie zum Vorschein oder // suggerieren // sie.«[30]

Die Skizzen der gehörnten Frau sind in der Regel undatiert, und die Figur ist horizontal und nicht, wie auf dem Umschlag von *Poésie sur Alger,* vertikal dargestellt. Eine datierte Skizze zeigt die *La femme à la licorne* gestützt von einer überdimensionierten Hand in aufrechter Haltung.[31] Interessanterweise ist im Hintergrund nicht die Stadt Algier zu sehen, sondern lediglich ein Küstenstrich – ein Hinweis darauf, dass der Plan noch nicht fertiggestellt war. Der Titel

– *Garder mon aile dans ta main* – ist ein Zitat aus einem Gedicht von Mallarmé.[32] Im Gegensatz zur Nacktheit der weiblichen Figur auf dem Cover ist die Kasbah in der Form einer Burka samt Schleier (Tafel 15) dargestellt, die Le Corbusiers Darstellung einer verschleierten Araberin (Abb. 6) nicht unähnlich ist.[33] Eine überdimensionierte, verschiedene nicht identifizierbare gebogene Formen haltende Hand[34] finden wir auch neben dem Text, in dem von der phönixhaften Wiederauferstehung Algiers und der Eroberung einer Höhe mithilfe einer stadtplanerischen Lösung die Rede ist[35] – eine Anspielung auf den Einfluss, den die Hand des Architekten auf die Lösung der Probleme Algiers hat: »Herr Bürgermeister, räumen Sie ein, dass dies keine Idee für die Zeit in hundert Jahren ist. Sie ist für jetzt und heute. Und als solche lässt sie sich in Einklang mit den zukünftigen Lösungen bringen, die Algier als Hauptstadt Afrikas [...] früher oder später ins Auge fassen muss.«[36]

Picasso, ein Künstler, den Le Corbusier außerordentlich schätzte, war offensichtlich ebenso fasziniert von den Algerierinnen, und es waren vermutlich die Wandgemälde von Le Corbusier in Cap Martin, die ihn zu seinen *Femmes d'Alger* inspirierten.[37] Die Serien mit Radierungen, die Picasso im Auftrag von Ambroise Vollard schuf, waren von Assoziationen

mit der *Corrida* und von der antiken Mythologie
(verkörpert durch die Figur des Minotaurus)
inspiriert. Vor allem zwei Radierungen erinnern
an Le Corbusiers gehörnte Frau: ein geflügelter
Stier mit weiblicher Brust und eine Vogel-
Frau.[38] Während Picasso den Stier feminisiert
und damit vermenschlicht, objektiviert Le Corbusier die weibliche Figur mit den ausladenden
Hüften und den prallen Brüsten in gewisser
Weise. Und während Picasso in den Vollard-
Radierungen den Künstler (also sich selbst) mit
dem Kopf eines griechischen Helden darstellt,
verkörpert Le Corbusiers überdimensionierte
Hand die künstlerische Kraft des Architekten.
Und auch zwischen Le Corbusiers *La femme
à la licorne* und Picassos Vogel-Frau und seinem geflügelten Stier gibt es eine Analogie,
nehmen beide doch indirekt Bezug auf die antike Mythologie.

Die übrigen Illustrationen der *Poésie* lassen
sich wohl am besten als grafische Collagen
aus schwarzer Tusche beschreiben, die hin und
wieder von blauen Farbklecksen überlagert
werden. Den menschlichen Aspekt suggeriert
das Auge, das der Künstler gelegentlich hinzu-
gefügt hat, während ein über dem Marinaviertel
schwebendes Flugzeug den Fortschritt symbo-
lisiert (Tafel 11). Mit allen ihm zur Verfügung ste-
henden Mitteln spiegelt Le Corbusiers kleines
Kunstbuch seinen wenn auch nicht unumstrit-

tenen visionären Ausblick auf das – urbane und künstlerische – Design wider. Wenn ein zeitgenössischer Architekt wie Jean Nouvel einräumt, dass »Architekten heute in hohem Maße eingeschränkt sind, weil sie nicht mehr in die wichtigen Entscheidungsprozesse einbezogen werden«, sagt dies viel über Le Corbusiers Zeit und über die Möglichkeit eines ganzheitlicheren Ansatzes in der Stadtplanung aus. Und Nouvel fährt fort: »Ich denke, sobald man nicht an einer Entscheidungsfindung beteiligt ist, die die Landschaft, die Farben, die Beziehung zu den anderen Gebäuden, den Kontext mit einbezieht, wird es keine wirklich interessanten Orte geben, denn dann macht jeder nur sein eigenes kleines Ding«.[39] Eine Beschreibung, die nur zu gut auf das London von heute zutrifft. Der idealisierte Plan zur Stadtgestaltung, den Le Corbusier für eine ihm im Grunde fremde Kultur ausgearbeitet hat, mag für Algier nicht die ideale Lösung gewesen sein, doch aufgrund der vielen Überlegungen und der vielen Zeit, die er in seine mögliche Realisierung investiert hat, hätte daraus unter Umständen etwas Revolutionäres entstehen können.

NACHWORT

Anmerkungen

1   Rowan Moore, »Eileen Gray's E1027: A Lost Legend of 20th-Century Architecture is Resurrected«, in: *The Guardian*, 2.5.2015.

2   Der vorliegenden Übersetzung liegt die in Rémi Baudouï (Hrsg.), *Poésie sur Alger – Histoire d'un Ouvrage,* Algiers 2013, veröffentlichte Textfassung zugrunde. Verweise auf die französische Originalausgabe beziehen sich, sofern nichts anderes vermerkt ist, ausschließlich auf diese Ausgabe. Der Vergleich des Niedergangs der Städte mit einer Krankheit ist eine Anspielung auf Albert Camus' 1947 erschienenem Roman *Die Pest*. In seinem Kondolenzbrief an die Witwe Camus' schrieb Le Corbusier: »Camus war 1931, 32, 33 in Algier Mitglied unserer Gruppe, zu einer Zeit, in der er sich auf ein unter Umständen gewagtes Abenteuer eingelassen hatte! Leider!« Fondation Le Corbusier (FLC), Korrespondenz mit Albert Camus.

3   Das innovativste Element des Wolkenkratzers waren die sogenannten »brise-soleil«, Sonnenblenden aus Beton, die ein direktes Eindringen des Sonnenlichts ins Gebäudeinnere verhindern.

4   Von dieser Ausgabe wurden 2525 Exemplare gedruckt, die ersten 25 auf Lafuma-Papier und die restlichen 2500 auf Alpha-Cellulose-Papier von der Papéterie du Marais.

5   »Langues Français–Anglais«, FLC 43-7 412.

6   An dieser Stelle möchte ich besonders Christine Mongin und Isabelle Godienau für die Unterstützung während meines Besuchs bei der Fondation Le Corbusier im Oktober 2014 danken.

7 Rainer Maria Rilke, *Lettres à un Jeune Poète,* erschienen bei Bernard Grasset, Paris 1941.

8   Le Corbusier, »Urbanisation de la ville d'Alger, 1931–34«, in: Le Corbusier, *Œuvre complète, 1929–34,* Zürich 1984, S. 174.

9   Zit. in Zeynep Çelik, *Urban Forms and Colonial Confrontations: Algiers under French Rule,* Berkeley und London 1997, S. 50. Zur Frage der Hygiene in den französischen Kolonien vgl. Cleo Cantone, »Senegal Rising: Emerging Anglophone Scholarship on Francophone West Africa«, in: *Canadian Jour-*

nal of African Studies, 2015, ttp://www.tandfonline.com/doi/abs/10.1080:00083968.2014.941201.

10 Baudouï 2013 (wie Anm. 2), S. 55.

11 Le Corbusier, »Urbanisation de la ville d'Alger, 1931–34«, in: Le Corbusier 1929–34 (wie Anm. 8), S. 24: »L'architecture arabe nous donne un enseignement précieux. Elle s'apprécie à la marche, avec le pied; c'est en marchant, en se déplaçant, que l'on voit se développer les ordonnances de l'architecture. C'est un principe contraire à l'architecture baroque qui est conçue sur le papier, autour d'un point fixe théorique. Je préfère l'enseignement de l'architecture arabe . . . Ils ont pu se loger si nombreux et à l'aise, dans les ombres diverses de la cour, dans l'espace des horizons de la terrasse, parce que cette architecture arabe détient le secret des dimensions humaines. Ces gens, ces guerriers terribles, aimaient a se reposer bien et entendaient gouter à la joie de vivre.« Die besondere Qualität der arabischen Stadtplanung erwähnt Le Corbusier auch in *Looking at City Planning,* New York 1963, S. 122.

12 Carl Gustav Jung, *Erinnerungen, Träume, Gedanken,* aufgezeichnet und hrsg. von Aniela Jaffé, Zürich und Düsseldorf 1985, Brief an Emma Jung, Sousse, 15.3.1920, S. 373–375.

13 Edward W. Said, *Power, Politics, and Culture: Interviews with Edward W. Said,* hrsg. und mit einer Einführung versehen von Gauri Viswanathan, New York 2002, S. 31.

14 Jung 1985 (wie Anm. 12), S. 248.

15 Poésie sur Alger (wie Anm. 2), S. 40.

16 Jung 1985 (wie Anm. 12), S. 242.

17 Ebd., S. 249.

18 Juan Calatrava und Winfried Nerdinger (Hrsg.), *Le Corbusier und das Gedicht vom rechten Winkel,* Ostfildern 2012, S. 109.

19 Le Corbusier, *Urbanisme projets A, B, C, et H (Alger), 1930–39* »ALGÉROIS, TA VOITURE NE PEUT PLUS CIRCULER PARCE QUE LE STATIONNEMENT ENCOMBRE TES RUES. IL

FAUT DONC T'INTERDIRE DE STATIONNER, MAIS ALORS TA VOITURE TE DEVIENT INUTILE ET INUTILES AUSSI SON VENDEUR, TON GARAGISTE, TON RÉPARATEUR, TON MARCHAND D'ESSENCE, TON ASSUREUR.«

20 Schreiben an den Bürgermeister von Algier, Le Corbusier 1929–34 (wie Anm. 8), S. 176.

21 Alexander von Segel, »Le Cheval de Troie du Bolchevisme«, zit. in: Jean-Louis Cohen, »A Journey through ›the Modern World‹«, in: Jean-Louis Cohen und Staffan Ahrenberg (Hrsg.), *Le Corbusier's Secret Laboratory – from Painting to Architecture,* Ostfildern 2013, S. 78.

22 Zeynep Çelik, »Le Corbusier, Orientalism, Colonialism«, in: *Assemblage* 17, 1992, S. 58–77.

23 Le Corbusier, »Le Folklore est l'expression fleurie des traditions«, in: *Voici la France de ce mois,* 16.6.1941, S. 31, zit. in: Çelik 1992 (wie Anm. 21), S. 62.

24 Poésie sur Alger (wie Anm. 2), S. 16: »Construisant leur Casbah (4), les Turcs avaient atteint au chef-d'oeuvre d'architecture et d'urbanisme.«

25 Zit. in: Marc Bérada, »La clef c'est: regarder«, in: Einführung zu Le Corbusier, *Voyage d'Orient, 1910–11,* Paris 2011, S. 11.

26 Stanislaus von Moos, *Le Corbusier – Elemente einer Synthese,* Frauenfeld und Stuttgart 1968, S. xxx.

27 Geneviève Hendricks, »Evocative Objects and Sinuous Forms: Le Corbusier in the Thirties«, in: Cohen und Ahrenberg 2013 (wie Anm. 20), S. 185.

28 Le Corbusier, *Quand les cathédrales étaient blanches,* Biarritz 1965, S. 22.

29 Ein gebogenes Horn, aus dem sich Geld in einen mit »caisse municipale« [Stadtkasse] beschrifteten Würfel ergießt, findet sich – als Anspielung auf die Vorzüge vertikaler Städte – in Le Corbusier 1929–34 (wie Anm. 8), S. 140. Eine spätere Skizze der Frau mit dem Horn trägt den Titel *Das Einhorn kommt vom Meer,* AVC, Charitable Foundation, Moskau, Gou-

ache und Bleistift auf Papier, in Cohen und Ahrenberg 2013 (wie Anm. 20), S. 235.

30 Le Corbusier, *Carnets (2) 1950–54,* Paris 1981, Nr. 707: »Cette idée (notion) de bestiaire humain m'est peut-être venue inconsciemment du contact si fréquent et à travers tout le monde et à travers toutes les couches sociales, avec les hommes et les femmes, dans les affaires, les comités, l'intimité. Les caractères apparaissant, qualifiant les sens et portant ou // proposant // leur typologie.«

31 Vgl. *Garder mon aile dans ta main,* 1946, Skizze, Buntstift, Tusche und Pastellkreide, 70 x 21 cm, Los-Nummer 108, versteigert am 26. September 2007 durch Zürichsee Auktionen, http://www.artvalue.com/auctionresult--le-corbusier-charles-edouard-j-garder-mon-aile-dans-ta-main-1637388.htm.

32 »Ô rêveuse, pour que je plonge
Au pur délice sans chemin,
Sache, par un subtil mensonge,
Garder mon aile dans ta main.«
Auszug aus »Autre éventail de Mademoiselle Mallarmé«, in: *Stéphane Mallarmé Poems,* Berkeley und Los Angeles 1957, S. 68.

33 Le Corbusier schuf eine ganze Reihe von Akt- und Halbaktskizzen – teilweise verschleierter – algerischer Frauen.

34 Poésie sur Alger (wie Anm. 2), S. 45.

35 Ebd., S. 44.

36 Le Corbusier 1929–34 (wie Anm. 8), S. 176.

37 Alan Read, *Architecturally Speaking: Practices of Art, Architecture, and the Everyday,* New York 2000, S. 150.

38 Stephen Coppard, *Picasso Prints – The Vollard Suite,* London 2012, Tafel 13, *Geflügelter Stier, von Kindern angestaunt,* Radierung, 1934, und Tafel 24, *Maskierte Figuren und Vogel-Frau,* Aquatinta und Radierung, November 1934.

39 Zit. in: Amelia Stein, »Jean Nouvel: ›Architecture is still an art, sometimes‹«, in: *The Guardian,* 15.5.2015.

Translation / Übersetzung
Cleo Cantone (English), Barbara Holle (Deutsch)

Copyediting / Lektorat
Irene Schaudies (English) / Karin Osbahr (Deutsch)

Project management / Projektmanagement
Karin Osbahr, Hatje Cantz

Graphic design and typesetting / Grafische Gestaltung und Satz
Gabriele Sabolewski, Hatje Cantz

Typeface / Schrift
Linotype Centennial, Bodoni Berthold BQ, Helvetica BQ, Times BQ

Production / Herstellung
Christine Stäcker, Hatje Cantz

Reproductions / Reproduktionen
Repromayer, Reutlingen

Printing / Druck
Offizin Scheufele, Stuttgart

Paper / Papier
Munken Print Cream 1.8, 115 g/m²

Binding / Buchbinderei
Verlags- und Industriebuchbinderei Nädele, Nehren

© 2016 for the reproduced works and the text by Le Corbusier /
für die abgebildeten Werke und den Text von Le Corbusier:
Fondation Le Corbusier, Paris

Published by / Erschienen im
Hatje Cantz Verlag
Zeppelinstrasse 32
73760 Ostfildern
Germany / Deutschland
Tel. +49 711 4405-200
Fax +49 711 4405-220
www.hatjecantz.com
A Ganske Publishing Group company /
Ein Unternehmen der Ganske Verlagsgruppe

Hatje Cantz books are available internationally at selected book-
stores. For more information about our distribution partners,
please visit our website at www.hatjecantz.com.

ISBN 978-3-7757-4096-8

Printed in Germany

The English part of this edition follows the original French edition
of 1950 in layout and typesetting. / Der englische Teil dieses
Buches lehnt sich mit dem Layout und Satz an die französischen
Ausgabe von 1950 an.